WINGS OVER GEORGIA

JACK CURRIE

LARGE PRINT

Oxford

First published in Great Britain 1989
by
Goodall Publications Ltd.

Published in Large Print 2010 by ISIS Publishing Ltd.,
7 Centremead, Osney Mead, Oxford OX2 0ES
by arrangement with
Crécy Publishing

British Library Cataloguing in Publication Data
Currie, Jack.
    Wings over Georgia. - - (Reminiscence)
    1. Currie, Jack.
    2. Great Britain. Royal Air Force. Bomber
Command.
    3. Air pilots, Military - - Great Britain - - Biography.
    4. World War, 1939–1945 - - Aerial operations,
British.
    5. World War, 1939–1945 - - Personal narratives,
British.
    6. Large type books.
    I. Title II. Series
    940.5'44'941'092–dc22

ISBN 978–0–7531–9558–1 (hb)
ISBN 978–0–7531–9559–8 (pb)

Printed and bound in Great Britain by
T. J. International Ltd., Padstow, Cornwall

WINGS OVER GEORGIA

Contents

BOEING-STEARMAN BIPLANE

The American Boeing-Stearman Model 75, on which the author S/Ldr. Jack Currie DFC did his primary flying training in the USA, was a highly successful training aircraft, no fewer than 10,346 being produced during World War Two. Several Marks of this two-seater trainer were produced for both the USAAF and the US Navy. Powered by a 220 hp Continental radial engine the aircraft had a maximum speed of 124 mph and a range of slightly over 500 miles.

The Stearman continues to be extensively flown in the USA, the Stearman Restorers' Association holding an annual National Stearman Fly-In at the Stearman HQ at Galesburg, Ill. A founder-member of The Arnold Scheme Register is a Director of a small group in England which owns one of these highly-regarded aircraft.

RAF AIRCREW TRAINING IN THE USA
1941–1945

For the greater part of the war, using facilities generously provided under "Lend-Lease" by the USA, the RAF was able to train aircrew at US flying schools far from the distractions of war-torn Britain. Even before the USA came into the war there was a refresher pilot training scheme in operation at four civilian flying schools in the US — two in California, one in Texas and one in Oklahoma — to assist American civilian pilots intending to volunteer for the RAF.

There were four distinct schemes in operation:

1. *The Arnold Scheme*
   Began early June 1941 by General Arnold of the US Army Air Corps. Early RAF classes arrived to enter civilian-run Primary flying training Schools but later classes first received acclimatisation/induction courses of varying duration to introduce them to US Army regulations and discipline before entering five other Primary schools. Two Army-run air bases provided Basic flying training, and five others gave Advanced flying training on single- and twin-engined aircraft, producing nearly 4,500 RAF pilots from over

7,500 original RAF entrants into The Arnold Scheme. Classes ended in February 1943.

2. *The Towers Scheme*
Began in July 1941 and ran until November 1944. The RAF used this scheme initially to train men for flying boats, although in 1943 some of the output was diverted to Bomber Command. The scheme also trained some Royal Navy aircrew, who then after getting their wings went on to do operational training at three locations in Florida, in preparation for operating on escort carriers. The numbers of pilots trained for the RN was in the region of 400 plus, as well as about 400 navigators and 660 wireless operators/air gunners.

3. *The BFTS Scheme*
Began in June 1941 and ran through until August 1945. There were six schools in all. A seventh was started but did not go beyond one primary course. No 1 at Terrell, Texas; No 2 at Lancaster, California; No 3 at Miami, Florida; No 4 at Mesa, Arizona; No 5 at Clewiston, Florida; and No 6 at Ponca City, Oklahoma; (No 7 operated briefly at Sweetwater, Texas). The size of courses at the BFTSs was initially around 50 per course (much smaller than those at the US Army schools) but were later doubled in size and for a time included a small number of US Army cadets. A number of RAF cadets, eliminated from The Arnold Scheme, were subsequently successful at BFTSs.

All the BFTSs were civilian operated and run with civilian American flying and ground instructors, and a small RAF supervisory staff.

Official records on the numbers of pilots produced for the RAF by the BFTSs, suggest a figure of some 7,000 plus.

4. *Pan-American Airways Observers' School*
Opened to RAF cadets in March 1941 and operated until October 1942. Initially based at Coral Gables, Florida, the flying was carried out at Dinner Key, south of Miami. The scheme produced approximately 1,300 navigators.

———————————

The Public Records Office at Kew shows that the total output provided by all American schemes combined was: Pilots — 13,673; Navigators — 1,715; and Wireless Operators/Air gunners — 662; a very considerable contribution to the Allied war effort.

The Publishers are indebted to Mr Bert Allam of No 1 BFTS Association, 5 Thornton Crescent, Old Coulsdon, Surrey CR3 1LJ, for the above information. Also Mr Norman Bate of the Arnold Scheme Register, 51 Henley Road, Leicester LE3 9RD for information regarding the Register history.

Foreword

After my first two books had been in circulation for a while, a number of people — well, three or four — wrote to ask if I planned to write the story of how I started in the RAF and learned to fly. The fact was that I had written something on those lines a year or so earlier, in a story called "The Way to Wickenby" (Wickenby was the airfield where I flew the Lancasters) but, when I'd shown it to my publisher, he hadn't liked it very much. He said that there were too many girls in it, not enough flying, and that the title wouldn't do at all. I might as well, he said, call it "Slow Train to Little Snoring". At that point, I'd dropped it, and got on with something else; however, when these people wrote, I read the manuscript again, and had to admit there was some substance in the criticism. I settled back into my corner of the George Hotel in Easingwold and, with the usual aid of forty-five gallons of draught Guinness, rewrote the story from the start.

Those earlier books tell the fate of some who feature in this story, and I know that of the rest some still survive. I hope that they, and other ex-"Kaydets", especially those who form the Arnold Register, will like what I have written. My thanks are due to Col. Stanley Marker, late of the USAF, and to the Albert F. Simpson Historical Research Centre, Alabama, for their help in topping up the memories of forty-seven years ago, and especially to Doctor Joe Tomberlin of Valdosta, Georgia — the sort of researcher and adviser writers dream about.

I can't pretend to have eliminated every last girl from the following pages — the careful reader may find the odd one cropping up here and there — but it's largely the story of how I learned to fly, and I take leave to dedicate it to the men who taught me: Wallace Bacon Sheffield and Lieutenant James M. Sena.

Jack Currie, Easingwold, Yorkshire, 1989

CHAPTER
ONE

The Trouble with Trig

"No pilot vacancies in the RAF, I'm afraid," said the Flight Lieutenant in the Edgware Recruiting Office. "You might try the Fleet Air Arm."

"I don't think they have any bombers," I said, "and that's what I want to fly."

He looked me over critically. "How old are you?"

"Eighteen."

"You don't look eighteen."

I wished I didn't have this tendency to blush when people doubt my veracity — especially when I was telling nothing but the truth. "Well, I am," I said. "Today's my eighteenth birthday, as a matter of fact."

"Hm. How's your trig?"

"I beg your pardon?"

"You need trigonometry to be a pilot — or an observer."

"Oh yes, trig," I temporised. "I might have to brush up on that a bit."

I'd scraped through arithmetic and geometry in Matric, but I knew as much trig as I did Japanese. I hurried home to mother, and she had the answer: one of her music pupils was a mathematics teacher, and would have as many lessons free as he gave me.

Breaking briefly from the sines, cosines and tangents, I took doe-eyed Joan to *Dawn Patrol* at the Dominion. Errol Flynn played the gallant Flight Commander, David Niven his debonair companion. The screen was full of RFC roundels and German crosses, goggles and gauntlets, scarves fluttering in the slip-stream and death-defying binges. Forgetful of the second feature and of Joan in the balcony — "I thought you'd gone to buy an ice," she remonstrated later — I walked down the stairway and into Station Road.

For several days I dreamed of high heroics, firing a clearing burst from the twin Vickers and squinting through my fingers for the Hun in the sun. In between dog-fights, I drove my father home from Acton and scraped a rear door-handle on the gatepost. Errol Flynn, I realised, would have avoided that. Then, true loyalty returned — the allegiance to the bomber I had felt since the Hendon Air Display of 1937, when Blueland's Wellesleys and Whitleys made their steady, menacing approach, through puffs of ack-ack and swarms of Hawker Demons, into the heart of Redland, and into mine.

"I think they've forgotten about me," I grumbled over breakfast. "I'm probably swotting all this beastly trig for nothing."

"I'm sure you're not, dear," said my mother. "Eat up your Grape Nuts."

In the short term, she was wrong. In two days at Cardington, in April 1940, they tested aptitude and comprehension, hearing and reflexes, stamina and eyesight, urine and blood. Of trig there was no sign, let alone a cosine. It was as though you had practised playing leg-breaks for hours, to find that no one bowled them at you in the match.

The sound of sobbing woke me in the darkness. Someone was far from home, and wished that he were not. I would have liked to comfort him, to say I knew just how he felt. One girl would have done that for another — boys, of course, could not. Before the sobbing ceased, I was asleep again.

Next afternoon, the sergeant in the Orderly Room offered me a pen. "Right," he said, "you've passed. Sign here for your railway warrant."

"Where am I going?"

"Home to Mummy. She'll be pleased to see you, I expect."

"You said I'd passed!"

He smiled tolerantly. "You're on Deferred Service. Just sign the book, will you?"

"What does it mean — Deferred Service?"

"For Chris' sake! It means your service is bloody deferred, what d'you think it means? We've got to find you a place at a training school. When we've done that, we'll have you, all right? Don't worry, Tiger, the war's going on for a while yet — you'll have bags of time to be a hero."

The problem of employment now arose. The occasional half-guinea from the *Harrow Observer* for a cartoon and the odd few shillings for a pseudo-Crosby vocal at a Saturday dance were not sufficient to support the humblest life-style. At the ARP post, the warden whom I served as a runner was sympathetic. "I seen it in the paper," he said, "where the Council's advertising for stretcher-bearers, down at the depot. You might as well hang about there as here, eh? And get paid for it, with a uniform and all."

"How much?"

"Two quid, two pound ten — better than a kick in the backside, anyway. And whatever it is, it's that much more than what you're getting now."

His arithmetic was sound, his reasoning irrefutable; he may also have wearied of keeping me in cigarettes. I signed on at the Council Offices and took the course in first-aid and elementary rescue. If you had come to me a fortnight later complaining of a broken leg, indulging in an epileptic fit or simply bleeding from an artery, I would have known — in theory — exactly what to do. Provided you didn't resist too much, I could have carried you downstairs and laid you on a stretcher. I knew the drill for stepping off in time with a fellow-bearer, for negotiating obstacles and loading on an ambulance. I would be almost sure to notice if you fell off the stretcher.

The ambulance and rescue teams at the Harrow and Wealdstone depot worked twelve hours on and twelve hours off, with daily training sessions which tended to interrupt the card games and the darts. There was a dormitory for the night-shift, and you could boil a kettle on the stove. Most people brought sandwiches, but my mother's rules required a hot, cooked meal, and I discovered Alf's Cafe, in an alley off the High Street.

The facade was not imposing, the interior was stark and the mainstream of lunchers passed it by, but a small clientele sat on wooden benches and ate a daily three-course meal for two shillings (one penny more for double jam with the roll).

To wait at table, Alf wore an off-white apron, carpet slippers and a mournful expression; his collarless shirt, with sleeves rolled to the armpit, was fastened by a bone stud at the neck. It was possible occasionally to glimpse the hands of "the Missus", offering a steaming plateful through the serving hatch, but for the most part she remained a disembodied voice, echoing the call for "Pie and two, twice", or "Baked jam, with". You didn't go to Alf's for female company, however, nor for scintillating small talk to the sound of a string quartet. Not that conversation was altogether lacking: Alf himself would occasionally rest bony knuckles on a table, pass a perfunctory cloth across its surface and deliver a comment on the conduct of affairs. "Bit of a fiasto in Norway, innit? Ole Chamb'lin wants ter git isself orf back ter Birmingham an' leave the job ter Winston, dunnee? You ain't ate all yer sprouts — in't they 'ot enough?"

This sort of criticism, as it transpired, was not confined to cafe society and, on 10th May, Neville Chamberlain handed over to Alf's nominee. The new National Government's Minister for Aircraft Production, Max Beaverbrook, promptly launched an appeal for scrap metal. Given enough old saucepans, he could build another Spitfire; enough iron railings, another Hurricane. To further the campaign, the ARP force

5

escorted a Spitfire mounted on a lorry through the streets of Harrow on a Saturday afternoon.

On such ceremonials, the drill was supervised by Sergeant Higgins (the rank had clung to him from military service), a rescue-team leader with a toothbrush moustache and short-cut hair who set an example on parade which we all tried to follow — all, that is, excepting Bert Stringer, to whom conformity was unacceptable and discipline unknown. Despite a hollow-chested stoop, the lank-haired Stringer stood over six feet tall, and he preferred to march among the smaller men, the better to draw attention to himself. Snuffling and giggling, he would slouch along, out of step and alignment, with a cigarette concealed in the palm of his hand. "Now then, Bert," the Sergeant would remark, "smarten up a bit and keep your dressing in the ranks." Stringer's response would be a squelching raspberry or a muttered obscenity, while the Sergeant, his weathered face a little darker of complexion, marched resolutely on.

Even by his own standards, Stringer's performance on the Spitfire parade was conspicuous: looking more than ever like the main attraction in a raree-show, he shambled along, gesticulating to the people on the pavement, now playing an imaginary trombone, now parodying a guardsman's strut. Our officer, proud and portly, marching in the front, saw none of this: Sergeant Higgins, at the rear, had all too clear a view.

Back at the depot, those of us on standby made for the rest room, taking off our helmets and passing cigarettes. Stringer, sprawling on a bunk, was embarking on a review of the parade when the door fell open with a crash. The Sergeant entered, hissing unpleasantly between his teeth, picked up a heavy rubber boot from a locker and commenced to belabour Stringer about the head, addressing him throughout in a quiet but forceful stream of expletives. Trying to protect himself with forearms and hands, Stringer squealed for mercy, but Higgins never paused in his assault. It occurred to me, and must have to others, that we were watching a man being beaten to his death. Some turned away, either through indifference or philosophical detachment, but luckily for Stringer others found it in their hearts to intervene.

Restraining hands were laid on Higgins, but the heavy boot still flailed, and some of those who held him felt its weight. At last he was overpowered, and a whimpering Stringer crawled away. Higgins carefully replaced the boot in the locker and straightened his tie. "Fancies hisself as a bit of a comedian, does Bert," he observed. "Trouble is, I ain't got no sense of humour."

It was from the rostrum of the Wealdstone dance hall that I first saw Marie. She had wide, blue eyes like a Christmas doll from Selfridges, and they were gazing up at me. A quick glance behind me revealed nothing of interest — only the drummer's knowing wink. No doubt about it, she was looking at me. I finished the song and stepped down from the stage. "Rather stuffy in here, don't you think? What about a breath of fresh air before the next number?"

She shook her head, and ripples of soft, blonde hair, touched her cheeks in turn. "The boy I came with — he's jealous already."

"Too bad."

She smiled, and asked where I worked. Floating in the warm blue pools she used for eyes, I told her. "But I'm just marking time there, you know. I'm going to be a pilot."

I had said that less to impress the girl than to reassure myself, for the months were going by. I met two school friends, both in uniform: their talk was of Whitleys and Wellingtons, Stirlings and Hampdens. I wrote a pleading letter to the Air Ministry in Kingsway, who suggested that I direct my query to the Recruiting Centre, Edgware. Six months hadn't changed the Flight Lieutenant: to call him a recruiting officer was to use a paradox. "I don't see what you're grousing about," he said. "You haven't passed the selection board yet."

"But," I protested, "the Sergeant at Cardington said . . ."

"You passed the aptitude and medical tests, that's all. The selection board's at Uxbridge — we'll let you know. Ask the next chap to come in, would you, as you leave."

I slunk back to Harrow, took the problem book to Wealdstone and recommended the swot.

In the depot yard, Marie smiled up from the wheel of an open Triumph Sunbeam. She wore a flat, peaked cap on the back of her head, and an open-necked khaki shirt. "Remember me? Can you come for a run?"

"Sorry," I said, "I'm on standby till eight. Is this your car?"

"'Course not, silly, it's Mummy's. I'll pick you up at eight, and we'll go somewhere for a drink — somewhere not too crowded."

The baby-blue eyes swept over me like searchlights, and the Sunbeam drifted away. Watching her go, I felt a sudden thrill, as though the skipper had said, "Get your pads on, you're in first." This would be an evening to remember — an unexampled breakthrough. Joan was a sweetie, but just too nice for what Marie put into mind; Sandy was a beauty, with her streamlined figure and her crisp, blonde curls — she could wallop me at tennis any time she liked but she tended to giggle if I tried another game; Hermione was glamorous and played a mean guitar, but she was terribly intelligent and mad about Marx — making love to Hermione would somehow seem profane.

No, if there were to be a journey into this secret, much-whispered region where I alone of my contemporaries (if they were to be believed) had yet to tread, it must be with this golden girl, Marie. When a check of cash in hand revealed rather less than half-a-crown, the name of Dicks sprang into mind — tall, bony Bob Dicks, with the shock of wire-wool hair and the gentle, growling whisper (a joint product of asthma and Woodbine cigarettes) which had often roused me in the dormitory with, "Psst, Jack! Wanna buy a battleship?" He was as close to being a friend as any at the depot and, as such, essential to the plan.

At ten minutes to eight, I put my overalls away. The Packard was hosed down and ready for the night-shift (the Council had, by now, decided I would do less harm driving an ambulance than loading it). Dicks would clock on in five minutes — in time to be bitten for a quid. But, as gunfire sounded in the east, like a prelude to the entrance of the Demon King, Sergeant Higgins strode towards me. "Now then, son," he said, taking my elbow in a powerful grip, "could I ask a favour?"

"Well, I'm just going off duty, but . . ."

"That's just it, son. That's where it lies, see."

"Where what lies, Mr Higgins?"

"It's Bob Dicks — just phoned in. Can't get in for a couple of hours yet — domestic matter, sickness in the home, something of that. If you was to take his duty till he comes, eh, son?"

The guns boomed louder as I walked back to the rest-room for the problem book: half-way through my nineteenth year, still waiting on the threshold, still unaware of what it was that lay beyond. The mysteries of trig had clearly to be solved, but, on that starlit, noisy night, I would rather have studied the mysteries of Marie.

Busy officers passed through the candidates' waiting-room at Uxbridge, and I scribbled sketches of them to while the time away. A Flight Lieutenant paused, and gave a hoot of laughter as he recognised a colleague. He took the pad away to "show the other chaps" and it was lying on the table when I sat before the board. "Can you do these to order?" asked the Chairman. "Go on, then, have a crack at me."

With a thought to my position, I should have drawn him as the finest-looking Squadron Leader in the RAF, but my pencil never seemed to work that way. It was clear that other members of the board found more amusement in the sketch than he, but he bore up pretty well. "Jolly good," he said, hardly snarling at all. "Don't you think so, Peter? As a caricature, of course." He turned the pad face down. "Right, I don't think we need keep you long, young man. Still in the same job, are you, part-time ARP?"

Unaware of what the consequences might be, conscious only of one more escape from trigonometry, I reported my advancement.

"Ambulance-driver? Full-time? Can't take you, then. I mean, you shouldn't really be here . . ."

I bleated a protest.

"Schedule of Reserved Occupations, nothing I can do. Sorry and all that." He handed me the sketch-pad. "Keep up the caricatures — we all need a bit of a laugh these days."

A laugh? I felt more like weeping as I travelled home to Harrow. "Don't worry, dear," said my mother, pouring tea. "I'll write to Mr Churchill. You remember how he raised his hat and smiled, when he came out of the Speech Room on the hill, just as we were passing? He'll put things right."

I knew better than to challenge this strange, maternal logic, but it did occur to me that, at this moment in our history, the Premier might have more pressing matters on his mind than those of one importunate RAF candidate. One would be the matter of the U-boats in the North Atlantic, which were sinking shiploads of material and food. There was less to eat in Britain as the months went by, and more of what there was had to be rationed. There were ways, it was rumoured, to supplement the coupons but, either there was no such venality in Whitmore Road or I knew nothing of it if there were. Committed to a battle with immovable bureaucracy, more determined daily to do unto the enemy as they were doing to us, I didn't take much notice of what went on around me. The ashen faces in the ambulance were other people's faces, the smouldering debris other people's homes. I drove where I was told to, following the vehicle in front. Twice I fell asleep behind the wheel when I turned off the ignition in the depot yard. My mother nodded when I mentioned this phenomenon. "That's to be expected," she observed, "when you stay up past your bedtime." It was a similar reaction to that she had shown on the first day of the war, when the sirens had sounded and I jumped on my bicycle to report to the warden's post. "Put your clips on, dear," she had ordered, "or you'll get oil on your trousers."

In mid-March a letter came from Edgware: the writer, who claimed to be my obedient servant, was glad to inform me that the Schedule of Reserved Occupations did not apply to volunteers for pilot training, and I should address myself to Uxbridge once again. Uxbridge, however, took a cautious view: my request to be released from the provisions of the Schedule would be referred to the Air Ministry for consideration. That writer, too, was my obedient servant: I was gathering a host of them, and still getting nowhere.

Three months went by, while over half the surface of the world men lived, fought and died — in the sands of Africa, the Mediterranean islands, Yugoslavia and Greece, in the valleys and hills of the Levant. Others died in darkened streets, in prison camps and cellars, in their factories and homes, in long pain or brief oblivion.

Then, late in June, the German Army invaded Soviet Russia, and the Luftwaffe's attentions were directed to the east. London had a respite from the bombers for a while. At the Wealdstone depot, we polished the vehicles, the equipment and the floors; we practised fire and gas drills and even played a game of cricket — Civil Defence versus the Police. It may be that the lull gave one of my obedient servants a chance to clear his "pending" tray (or maybe Mr Churchill read my mother's letter): whatever the cause, I had a call from Uxbridge to report for attestation. "I'm on the day-shift," I said, "but I'm off on Sundays — can I come then?"

"Nothing to stop you coming, but there won't be anyone here. We like to have a day off too, you know. You could go to Weston-super-Mare, I suppose — they work seven days a week down there."

13

I caught an early train from Paddington, and arrived in Weston at midday. In an otherwise deserted office-block, a corporal and an AC2 were playing darts. "Swearing in," observed the Corporal, taking careful aim, "needs an officer. There's only the one on duty of a Sunday, and he'll be having his dinner." He pencilled his score on the wall beside the dartboard. "You might as well fill the form in. Sniffy, give him a twenty-one sixty-eight."

Working quickly through the paper, I declared I'd never married, been convicted by a court or a member of any other service of the Crown. At the question, "What is your trade or calling" I sucked the pen and pondered. If I answered "Ambulance Driver", the whole rigmarole might begin again. I wrote "Cartoonist", and signed the form.

It was past two o'clock when the officer returned, pink-cheeked and affable, in excellent spirits with himself, with his lunch and all the world. He offered me a chair. "Done the paperwork — the old bumph? Jolly good." He ran a finger down the form. "That seems all right. Hope so, anyway, otherwise you're liable for two years in the clink, with hard labour." He laughed heartily, and donned his cap. "Right, hop up, old thing. Grab hold of the good book and sing out what it says on the card."

Taking the Bible and a deep breath, I swore by Almighty God to be faithful and bear true allegiance to His Majesty King George VI, his heirs and successors; in duty bound, honestly and faithfully, to defend the same, in person, Crown and dignity against all enemies;

to observe and obey all orders of the same and of the air officers and other officers set over me, so help me God.

"Spoken like a scholar and a gentleman," chuckled the officer, taking off his cap and unbuttoning his tunic. "No need to look so grim, old thing — you're in the Royal Air Force now!"

CHAPTER
TWO

Bernoulli and
Bill the Bastard

A month later, I was one of sixty u/t pilots who formed three ranks in front of Stratford-upon-Avon's Shakespeare Hotel while a squat, swarthy Corporal regarded us with an expression of implacable hostility. He gave an order in a tone which Captain Bligh might have employed to call for fifty lashes. "Flight, stan' at . . ." The words echoed to and fro among the buildings, and he paused, as a few unwary left feet moved. "As you were," he snarled. "Do not anticipate the word of command, you horrible people!"

If we really did seem horrible to him, the seeming was, on my part, entirely unintentional: my sole purpose was to exist from day to day, as inconspicuously as possible, until life evolved into a recognisable, human pattern and, as it surely must, improved. Since I took the oath at Weston and arrived at Arsey-Tarsey (ACRC, the Aircrew Reception Centre), I had been buttoned and buckled into rough, blue serge, strapped into a webbing belt and harness, loaded with kitbags full of strange impedimenta, and hung about with

16

water-bottle, back-pack, side-packs, gasmask and dixie. Cringing groups of us had visited the barber — "Your usual trim, Sir?" — and emerged so depilated that our mothers wouldn't know us; antibodies had been stimulated in our systems by the injection of dead germs, toxides and calf lymph; blood had been syphoned from our veins and its category dye-stamped on the fireproof tags which hung around our necks.

We had been lectured to and shouted at by nameless tyrants; we had marched — not very well, because we didn't know how — along the streets of St John's Wood, through Regent's Park and, to the amusement of the occupants, past the monkey houses at the Zoo, behind the stands at Lord's, through which another, better world could occasionally be glimpsed, and back through the streets to Bentinck Court.

Now, at No 9 Initial Training Wing, Stratford, we had found a Corporal who liked us even less than his London equivalents. "What I can see," he remarked, in what for him was an undertone, "is that I gotta lotta work on with you people. Let's try again. Flight, stan' at — ease!"

The "ease" was a shriek. A herd of elephants, chancing to pass through Stratford, would have recognised it instantly, and charged. Left boots clattered on the roadway like a salvo from a drunken firing party. The Corporal raised his eyes skyward and uttered a blasphemy. "Stand — easy!" Thumbs hooked under the flaps of his breast pockets, he paced slowly along the front rank. "Right. I am your Corporal. My friends call me 'Bill', but you people will at all times address me as 'Corporal'. You may hear me referred to as 'Bill the Bastard', and it is true that I can be — that I have it in me to be — a bit of a bastard. If I have to be." He faced us, smiling balefully, before continuing in a soft, caressing tone. "I hope I do not have to be — for your sake. All you have got to do is remember this: I am, in fact, your best friend. If you play ball with me, I will play ball with you. All right?"

The murmur of assent left him unsatisfied: he repeated the question on a rising note. "Yes, Corporal," we screeched.

"Right. Now that we understand each other, we will proceed to your airmanship lecture. To save you having to walk, I will march you there. And I want you to march in a smart and airmanlike fashion. I do not want my Flight to be a disorderly rabble in the streets of Stratford: I want my Flight to be the smartest Flight in the whole bloody Wing. That is what I want: that is what I will have. Right?"

"Yes, Corporal!"

He unhooked his thumbs and, at attention, stared over our heads as though seeking inspiration. Finding it, he resumed his elephant impression: "Flight! Oh, Christ — as you were. When I give you 'Flight', that is a precautionary word of command. On that word, you will assume the 'At ease' position — shoulders back, head erect, arms straight, left thumb in the palm of the right hand. Flight! That is better — slightly better. Ah — ten — shun! Move to the right in column of route. Right — turn! By the left, quick — march! 'Ef — 'ight — 'ef — 'ight — 'ef . . . 'ef . . ."

The airmanship lecturer was a stiff-faced, pale young man with the rank of Pilot Officer, and although I was aware that there were many such who weren't really pilots, just as there were Flying Officers who didn't fly and Flight Lieutenants who never made a flight, it seemed rather strange that a teacher of that subject had no air experience. That, however, was no fault of his, and he certainly excelled in one area — as a boredom-maker he really stood alone. It couldn't have been easy to talk for an hour about the theory of flight and expunge it entirely of colour and excitement, but he contrived to do so with no difficulty at all. In his hands, the conquest of the air — man's attempt to emulate the eagle — became a blackboard diagram of interacting forces, a chalked rectangle of lift, thrust, weight and drag.

For our Pilot Officer flight occurred because of certain laws of motion, scientifically established many years before the brothers Wright were born. Air, for example, flowing across a cambered surface (say, an aircraft wing), tended to accelerate and make the surface lift: Bernoulli made a point of this, and Venturi backed him up. All you had to do was give the surface thrust (e.g. with an engine) to make the air flow over it. So far, so good. But then you had to take account of Newton, who tiresomely observed that to each and every action comes an equal and opposite reaction: the more the engine thrust you forward, the more the air would drag you back. And Newton also took the view, essentially bad news for flying men, that bodies in the

19

atmosphere are influenced by weight, which acts in the general direction of down.

This much I hoisted in, but my juvenile reaction was "so what?" I needed no convincing that aeroplanes could fly, nor reasons why they actually should not. They did, and that was that. There was no point in arguing about it. But many of these lectures, and others that were given in those two months at Stratford, seemed ill-conceived to me. Bernoulli and company were clearly first-class chaps, and pretty hot at physics, as were Boyle and Charles on engines, and Oersted, Ohm and Faraday on electricity, but to the aspiring pilot who had yet to see an aircraft at close quarters, theirs was esoteric, academic stuff. If it were your aim to turn a sturdy schoolboy into a fast bowler, you wouldn't read him a lecture in ballistics before he wore a pair of flannels: you would feed him beefsteak and put a ball in his hand.

But there was not much to complain of and a lot to be thankful for at No 9 ITW. We lived in a fine hotel where we ate as well as most, and better than many in the British Isles in 1941. I was paid half-a-crown a day (occasionally supplemented by a postal order from my father, when the mood fell upon him or in answer to a plea), and deserved nothing more: aircraftmen, second class, were no use to anyone, as we were frequently reminded, nor ever likely to be if we didn't smarten our ideas up. We had no expenses, and we were free to spend our income totally on pleasure. True, we worked ten hours a day for six days a week, but we made the most of our leisure, either at the Memorial Theatre, or boating on the river or simply getting to know each other over ersatz coffee at the Judith Shakespeare Cafe or mild-and-bitter at the "Mucky Duck".

It was this intercourse with the hearts and minds of others that was the best part, for me, of the ITW experience. The comradeship and humour of the men at Wealdstone had been enjoyable, but they were of another generation and they hadn't shared my goal. My class-mates' company was a lot more congenial. There were those such as prim Ronald Featonby, the Foreign Office clerk, big Jim Skinner, with the style of a country squire's favourite son, Ron Treadaway from Dorset and Mac McLeod, the black-haired Highlander, who were very like the boys I'd known at school. The lantern-jawed comedian, Mugsy Johnson from Edmonton, Percy Burt from Clapham and Jim Withers from Waltham didn't differ greatly from the local lads in Harrow. Scotty Walker, however, with the lightning repartee and Glasgow urchin's face, Harry Lawton from Higham Ferrers ("Where? Never heard of it."), and Dave Garrett, the fairground pugilist from Bristol, were of an unfamiliar breed, and fun to get to know.

We had these things in common: we were sound in wind and limb, we had achieved the requisite standard of formal education and we wanted to fly. And now we were on our way: the RAFVR badge on our shoulders and the white flash in our caps told the world that we were aircrew under training. There was a mutual spirit of endeavour among us and each wanted the others to succeed. No rivalry existed — that would come later, when places were limited at the next stage of flying, and there had to be a weeding-out among the ranks. But we didn't know that then: and if there were any sort of competition at Stratford, it was among the sycophantic few who vied with one another for Bill the Bastard's favour.

That this fell on me, willy-nilly, was due to an unexpected aptitude in the subject which was the Corporal's responsibility and closest to his heart — I actually enjoyed the rhythm of foot-drill and arms-drill, and the measured ritual of marching on parade. Noticing this, he entrusted me with preparing D Flight for his coming, and with moving it from here to there when he, himself, did not feel so inclined.

This favoured position, however, brought no immunity from the wrath of other Corporals — certainly not from that of PTIs. The trouble was that, unlike drill, physical training in any of its forms did not appeal to me at all. I had detested it at school and liked it no more now. There were those in the Flight who actually enjoyed it, and others who didn't, and yet made every effort to emasculate themselves on vaulting horses, to run across country to the point of collapse, and to perform contortions at a PTI's command which would have made an orang-utang think twice. The Creator had cast me in a different mould: whenever a PTI sang out the words "With me, begin!" I simply and devoutly wished I were not there.

The wish, as a previous Stratfordian had put it, was father to the thought, and the thought was simple — as good thoughts often are. I would take up a position at the rear of the Flight as it neared the PT shed and, as

22

the last file trooped inside, quietly walk away. In the event of a roll-call by the PTI an accomplice would give a yelp of "Sir" in answer to my name (it was a fiction of the ritual that an officer was present). It only remained to find a volunteer: Walker, although keen to help, had an accent which, even with a monosyllable, was quite unmistakable, as was Garrett's husky growl; Featonby had trouble with his moral scruples. Johnson, Burt and Skinner, however, were budding ventriloquists, and McLeod was reliable in all affairs which held an element of anarchy.

The coalition of accomplices had happened spontaneously, for no specific reason, unless it was in self-defence against the regime that, in all Service training schools, set a gulf between the teachers and the taught, the oppressors and oppressed. We hadn't chosen one another because we'd found ourselves together on parade, in the classroom or the dining hall. We came from different backgrounds, spoke in different accents, had different likes and dislikes. It can't have been simply that we shared a sense of humour, for Featonby had none, and Skinner very little. If it wasn't just chance that had melded us together, it must have been some sort of empathetic instinct. But however those early friendships started — and ours was only one of such groupings in the Wing — the fact was that most of them survived for a lifetime. Admittedly, some of those lifetimes weren't very long.

In contrast to the wealth of masculine companionship, female company was scarce. The bomber crews from Wellesbourne Mountford had the pick of what there was, as was right and proper, indeed inevitable, with their rank and flying badges, and the permanent staff of the ITW naturally had a lien on the rest. Featonby, however, to the group's surprise, contrived to strike up an acquaintance with a girl called Rhoda, who worked in the Post Office. She had long, black hair, a beautiful figure, and was cool and rather snooty, as was Featonby himself. He brought her into the Mucky Duck and stood at the bar with a smirk on his face. He had recently shaved and applied some unguent to his hair. Walker cast an eye over Rhoda and made a low, snarling noise. Featonby asked what she would care to drink.

"Vodka, please, Ronald."

"Vodka?"

"It's a Russian drink, you know — they have it here."

"Oh, vodka," said Featonby. "Of course. Two vodkas, please."

He turned to me and simulated a start of recognition — as I knew he would. From tiny roots, the friendship had quickly developed its own character and form. "My room-mate," he explained to the girl, and offered me a drink.

"Vodka will be fine, thanks, Ron."

He frowned slightly, and glanced at the others. "You fellows are in your own school, I expect."

They looked at each other blankly. "Of course," said McLeod, "if you'd rather we went somewhere else . . ."

Featonby summoned a smile. "Not at all." He explored his purse with a finger. "Mild and bitter, is it?"

"Vodka's ma favourite," Walker admitted.

"Mine, as well," said Lawton.

"We usually sup vodka," Burt remarked, "in The Plough at Clapham."

Garrett raised a fist in salute. "Up the Russkis!"

"A toast to the Red Army," said McLeod. "Jolly good show!"

Featonby extracted a note as though he were pulling a plaster off an open wound. "That'll be eight vodkas altogether, please, Miss."

Rhoda swung a dark wave of hair off her cheek, and tossed the drink down at a gulp. Attempts to follow her example produced an outbreak which would have excited comment in a doctor's waiting-room during the great influenza epidemic. Rhoda gave a tinkling laugh. "I can see," she said, "that you don't know how to drink vodka."

We rallied to her side. "Will ye no show us the trick of it," suggested Walker, "if Ron gets you another?"

Featonby, dabbing his eyes with a handkerchief, drew her away. "There's a table for two over there," he said, and looked down his nose. "I'll see you fellows later."

I wrote a letter home, describing an excursion on the Avon, reporting a pass in the mid-course exams and mentioning that Leslie Ames, the England wicket-keeper, was our Officer i/c Sport. I revealed, in passing, that there was not a cigarette to be had in all of Stratford. My father responded with a page of guidance for the rowing man, two packets of Players', and an instruction to make myself known, as a fellow-cricketer, to Flight Lieutenant Ames. He added his blessing.

Featonby and I smoked the cigarettes and practised feathering our oars. As for Mr Ames, you could only talk to an officer if an NCO was present, and I foresaw a difficulty in convincing Corporal Bill of a need for the encounter. Furthermore, experience of approaching great cricketers (apart from Yorkshire players, who treated you as family if you wore the County tie) hadn't been encouraging: on seeking autographs at Lords in 1934, as they left the field for lunch, Woodfull had ignored me, Kippax had frowned and Bradman had succinctly answered "No".

My mother returned a parcel of washing (you had to do your own at Stratford, and I was unprepared for that), with a letter. "We are supposed," she wrote, "to have a tear-gas test in Harrow within the week. It was arranged for Saturday afternoon but the Police objected. I hope Hitler has taken note." She had taken Sandy — the only girl on my list of whom she approved — to see *Lady Hamilton* at the Dominion, and wished I had been with them.

I wished so, too, but even with the wings which were my goal, I couldn't have made it, for every evening of that week I was otherwise engaged. The reason for this had been hunger, simple hunger, brought on, undoubtedly, by over-exertion. "Now we know we can do twenty press-ups," the PTI had chanted, "we'll start this lovely morning off with thirty, shall we? Come along, that dozy man, you can do better than that — force yourself! And, press . . ."

That agony over, we had marched for miles into the country for Aldis lamp practice — flashing meaningless streams of letters and numbers at each other across the sodden fields; then back to the classrooms for arithmetic, and engines, and stripping Browning guns; to the cinema, for a film about unmentionable diseases, guaranteed to put you off your lunch — if not sex — for ever; to the armoury for rifles, and "Order arms, slope arms, present . . . port . . . trail . . ."

The evening meal was served at half-past five, and by twenty-two hundred hours anyone not suffering from anorexia nervosa was liable to be ravenous. Walker prowled the bedroom like a tiger. "Doon in the Sergeants' kitchen," he growled, from the corner of his mouth, "there's grub for the taking. There's bread and jam and cake and wee pots of meat-paste and . . ."

"What do you mean, for the taking?" asked McLeod, pushing his cap to the back of his head (unlike most of us, he was devoted to the forage cap, and only removed it in class, church or bed). "They don't just leave it lying around, do they?"

"As good as. Och, it's in the larder, but that's no locked — well, no properly locked."

I buttoned my tunic, and kicked Featonby's bed. "What about it, Ron? Raiding party?"

He turned a page of his Penguin paperback. "Certainly not. I'm not jeopardising my record for a slice of bread and jam."

"Pots of meat-paste, eh?" mused McLeod.

"And tins of treacle, and cocoa — and, aye, a bloody great jar of rum."

We were quick and we were cautious; our night-vision was good; Walker, feline in his movements, had no trouble with the lock. We covered our tracks carefully, and crept back with the booty.

The Flight, next morning, stood in open order after Corporal Bill's inspection, when the hotel doors opened and the Sergeant stood before us. A neat, smooth-faced man, he was seldom seen, except perhaps on church parade or leaning on the desk of the hotel when he was Orderly Sergeant. This rare sight of him was made rarer yet by the fact that he carried, in the crook of his arm, a four-pound tin of jam.

Corporal Bill crashed to attention. "D Flight present and correct, Sarn't," he screeched.

The Sergeant came straight to the point. "This," he said, tapping the lid, "is a tin of jam — plum and apple jam, in point of fact — from the Sarn'ts' Mess." He paused, looking down at the tin, as a ventriloquist might draw attention to his dummy. "Last night," he continued, "so the NCO i/c informs me, it was a full tin of plum and apple jam. This morning, however, it is not full. It is, in point of fact, half empty." He glanced into the tin. "Approximately half empty. The NCO i/c also informs me that certain other commodities are missing from his shelves."

He glanced at Corporal Bill, who marched to his side and accepted the tin as though it were the object of a formal presentation. "It would appear," said the Sergeant, "that some naughty person or persons has been doing a bit of pilfering. What I want to know is, who that naughty person or persons might be."

There was a low murmur in the ranks, little more than an exhalation of breath, as though a herd of cattle sensed the coming of the slaughterman. "Silence on p'rade," snarled Corporal Bill. "Stand perfickly still!"

"It would probably be best," said the Sergeant, "if that person or persons were to own up — stand forward and own up, immediately. Otherwise . . ."

He embraced us in a long, slow gaze, and we all knew what was coming: punishment of the innocent for the crime of a few. It had happened to subject groups before — it was probably happening in Europe even now. ". . . otherwise, I shall have to cancel all privileges for the whole Flight for a fortnight, and I'm sure the Corporal will find you something horrible to do." He smiled, engagingly. "What about it, lads? Whoever did it knows he did, right? The only question is, is he man enough to own up?"

Half a mile away, an errand boy was whistling; a little further off, someone slammed a door. The Sergeant glanced at his watch. McLeod, judging his moment, and looking like a throwback to Sidney Carton or Beau Geste, took a pace to the front. "I'm the one to blame, Sergeant."

"Me too, Sarge," said Walker, also stepping forward.

"Me too, *Sergeant!*" Corporal Bill amended, automatically. The Sergeant looked at him blankly, and he gulped. "I don't mean me too, Sarn't, I mean him too, Sarn't."

"You had me worried for a moment, Corporal," said the Sergeant. The tension broke into fragments of laughter. I added my confession, followed by Featonby. The Sergeant nodded. "Take these people's names, Corporal, and charge them. Carry on."

"Spot of jankers for you lot," said Corporal Bill, as the Sergeant retired to the hotel. "Oh, my word, yes." He wrote our wicked names in his little, black book and put it back into his pocket. "Flight, close order — march. Right — dress."

Arms were extended to touch the next man's shoulder, feet shuffled back and forward until the lines were straight. "What did you do that for, you twirp?" I hissed at Featonby. "You didn't pinch any grub."

"I know that," he muttered crossly. "But I ate some."

"Eyes front," roared the Corporal. "As you were! I wanna see those arms come down smartly. I want your heads and eyes to move like a flash of lightning. Gawd blimey, you're getting sloppy. Eyes — front!"

It was our first offence, and the sentence wasn't harsh. Seven days CC — which was purely nominal, for there was no camp to be confined to — and seven days defaulters' parade. Each evening we stood outside the Guard Room with the night-duty airmen; the Orderly Corporal lowered the flag and despatched us to our penal tasks. "Defaulters stand fast, guard and fire picket, to the right, to your duties — dismiss. Defaulters, follow me."

While McLeod and Featonby scoured tins in the Sergeants' Mess kitchen, Walker and I scrubbed the dining-room floor. The Mess Corporal grinned as he handed us the buckets and brushes. "Never mind, lads, eh? I mean, till you done some jankers, you don't know you've joined."

CHAPTER
THREE

One More Stall for Luck

"Throttle set," said the instructor, "mixture lever set, fuel-cock on, switches off." All I could see of him, as he sat in the front seat of the Tiger Moth, bulky and relaxed, was the back of his helmet and the turned-up collar of an Irving jacket. His words came through the Gosport tube into the earphones of my helmet, which was as new, clean and splendid as the rest of the kit: the Sidcot inner suit, like a man-sized silken quilt, and the outer, of heavy, pale-grey canvas; suede, fur-lined boots over thick, woollen socks; two pairs of gloves, white silk and woollen, covered by leather gauntlets, reaching halfway to the elbow.

All this outfit, with the goggles and the underwear, required a kitbag to itself, and u/t aircrew on the move could always be identified by the fact that they carried two bulging kitbags whereas sensible airmen only carried one. We found that it was best to hoist the heavier on one shoulder and drag the other by the neck (people who tried to carry one on each shoulder tended to walk into obstacles or to get lost in transit). The snag was that this, in time, made one arm longer than the other, and sartorially-conscious airmen would find throughout their lives that jackets off the peg were not for them.

It wasn't only kit that we had gained on arrival at No 10 Elementary Flying School, Ansty: pay had increased to three half-crowns a day, and rank from AC2, the lowest of the low, to Leading Aircraftman — we were folding our arms at every opportunity to see the propeller badges on our sleeves.

Now, cocooned in the heavy kitbag's contents, I sat in the Tiger Moth's rear cockpit and, for Featonby's sake (he was next man on board and watching me closely), tried hard to maintain an air of nonchalance, while awaiting my first experience of flight. It was almost two years since the officer at Edgware had greeted me with such heartfelt apathy: this flying instructor seemed equally unmoved. His manner was dispassionate and matter-of-fact, his voice a practised drawl. "Make yourself comfortable, and keep a good lookout for other aircraft. Follow me through on the controls."

Already we had entered into that relationship that would recur in training many times, and this one had a special significance: I might be Wreford's hundredth pupil, or five-hundredth, but he would always be my first flying instructor, and his would be the name at the top of page one of my first log-book. He would probably forget me in a month, but I would remember him, and the back of his head, for ever.

I felt the joy-stick and the pedals responding to his touch, saw the throttle-lever advancing in its quadrant as he taxied forward on the grass. The undercarriage wheels — (no bigger than a fairy-cycle's) — set up a rumbling vibration in the flimsy fuselage. To see the way ahead on each side of the nose, he swung the rudder sharply to make a zig-zag path across the field. At the downwind boundary, he throttled back and stopped, broadside on to the light November wind.

While he called out the take-off checks, another Tiger Moth, its propeller windmilling, floated down in front of us, bounced once and settled, wheels and tail-skid together, and ran on along the landing strip. Wreford released the brake and turned the nose into the wind. This was the moment, long awaited, not to be forgotten . . . but not yet. The aircraft stopped. More checks. The sky was beckoning, a bright pale blue, and as clear as water. No gauge, no instrument, no technicality should be allowed to keep us from it. We knew enough about this aeroplane — the engine answered to the throttle, the rudder to the pedals, the ailerons and elevators responded to the stick — what more was there to know? All right, you could possibly make doubly sure the petrol was turned on and, if you must, reassure yourself about the compass setting — but please, Mr Wreford, no more of your patter, don't let your instructional technique destroy the magic! Please be quiet, and please be quick — just get this Tiger Moth up into that sky!

Unhurriedly, the pontiff turned his head to left and right, waving an explanatory hand, still talking. The slipstream tore a word or two away — I let them go. Then, beside me, on the left side of the cockpit, the throttle-lever moved; the aircraft trembled as it strained against the brakes, and I knew how it felt. Then, it rumbled forward, the lever reached its stop, the tail-skid left the grass, and we were running on the wheels — straight and true and faster, ever faster. I felt the rudder pedals move as Wreford maintained that straight, true line, felt the Gipsy Major engine give the utmost of its power in the fight to overcome the friction of the grass and the airflow that conspired to hold us back. The slipstream beat against the canvas, whistled through the rigging wires and howled at the struts, making such a din that I almost missed the moment when the wheels no longer rumbled and the Tiger Moth was flying.

I looked back at the airfield where the buildings were receding and foreshortened in the shadows of the low-lying sun. The landscape tilted as Wreford banked the aircraft and, instinctively, I clutched the stanchions of the seat. The Sutton harness-straps pressed against my shoulders — I relaxed and leaned into the turn.

To the west lay Coventry, still showing the wounds inflicted a year ago; to the east ran the Oxford Canal, the railway track from Rugby, and the straight stretch of road that bisected Ansty village. The sky I saw from six hundred feet was the same I had seen from six feet on the airfield, but there was much more of it, in every direction — it was like being on a mountain-top without the mountain — and I could feel it, ice-cold on my cheeks, tugging at my collar.

I pulled the helmet's chin-strap tighter and, as Wreford had ordered, set my feet on the pedals and my fingers on the stick, but I couldn't associate, at that remove, their movements with the way the aeroplane behaved — it was like putting your hands on a pianola's keyboard and pretending you were playing. You had to have control yourself, and the intention, to match the cause with the effect.

On the panel in front of me were the blind-flying instruments — ASI, altimeter, compass, artificial horizon and climb-and-descent indicator. At least I could feel some physical affinity with the last of these: the upper needle leaned into the turn, as I had done, and the lower needle pointed at the bottom dead centre, the way my behind was pressed into the seat.

Occasionally the aircraft twitched its nose from side to side, tipped a wing, or fell a few feet — as though, for a moment, it had forgotten how to fly. I began to realise that the air in which we moved was never still, but moving too, rocking the Tiger Moth, jolting it, nudging it off course from time to time.

I was trying to absorb this experience, to understand what it meant and, essentially, to credit that it was happening to me, when Wreford returned to the airfield's traffic pattern. Ten minutes was enough, according to him, for an "Air Familiarisation" detail. Nor was it Ansty's role, he said, taxiing round the airfield to the pickup point, to teach someone to fly in record time: it was to lead him, in five hours or so, to the verge of solo flight and, on the way, to discover those who had a tendency to sickness in the air or

35

whose co-ordination, aptitude, whatever, though good enough to pass the Cardington tests, lacked something that was needed, and only could be tested, in the air.

My mother, unaware of the largesse of the flying-clothing stores, sent knitted gloves and socks, and the local news: one of my friends was flying a Boston, one had joined the Navy, two were POWs, and the Braund twins — John and Paul — had sailed overseas for pilot-training, but whether to Canada, South Africa or America, was unknown. The singing trig instructor had been gratified to learn of my navigation marks at Stratford (99% had secured joint first place with Amar Singh, the Sikh whose accent was more English than the English and whose strange devotions, and unwinding of the turban, I had watched with fascination in the Bentinck Court dormitory). In conclusion, she urged me to be sensible and to take no unnecessary risks. (Another trainee's mother had been more specific: her son, she adjured him, was to be sure he always flew low and very slowly.)

In the days that followed that first ten-minute detail, Wreford taught me how to taxi, take off into wind, climb, fly straight and level, turn left and right, recover from a stall, and make a glide-approach and landing. He had demonstrated each exercise in progression, and I had copied him, over and over, until I got it right. To fly the Tiger Moth was easy — it responded to the touch like a well-oiled bicycle — to fly it to Wreford's satisfaction, holding the airspeed steady on the climb, rolling smoothly into the turns, with exactly the right balance of rudder and stick to keep that lower needle at bottom dead centre, was not. The circuits, too, had to be accurate: strict rectangles, with the first right-angled turn at 600 feet on the climb after take-off, the second at a thousand to fly the down-wind leg, and the third to turn cross-wind as soon as the wing-tip passed the downwind boundary fence. At first, that seemed much too close to the airfield, but, what with the wind and the out-throw of the turn, it put the aircraft at the right place in the sky to make turn number four, on to the approach.

Once there, you throttled back and let the speed fall off, directing the nose at the touch-down point. If the wind blew the aircraft off the approach line, the instinctive reaction was to redirect the nose towards that point. Wrong: it would put you on a parallel track, downwind of the right one, the wind would keep on blowing, you would keep on turning, and eventually be faced, at best, with a downwind landing. At worst, you would emulate the Oozlum bird, which was reputed to fly in ever-decreasing circles until it disappeared up its fundamental orifice. The right thing to do was to double the angle you first thought of, get back on line and, when you were, turn through half the angle back the other way. Then all you had to do was to judge the height correctly, hold the aircraft two or three feet above the grass, pull the stick back gently — right back — and hold it, hold it, keep straight with the rudder and — plop! You heard the rumble of the wheels, felt all the little furrows in the field and knew that you had made another happy landing.

All this was playing with the forces of which the cold-eyed instructor at Stratford had spoken: you were eliminating thrust by shutting off the throttle, balancing lift and drag with the elevators, and letting Sir Isaac have his way with the rest. Wrefold had shown what would happen when we practised stalling, at a safe 4,000 feet: he had pulled up the nose until there was nothing to see but sky, nothing to hear but the whisper of the airflow, and nothing to feel but sympathy for the aircraft as it tried to keep on flying — it was like the moment, on a fairground swing, when you reach the limit of its travel, just before it starts to drop. The aircraft sank a little, trembled, the nose fell like an axe and suddenly the view ahead changed from sky to most of Warwickshire. Wreford waited until the speed built up, and climbed away to do it all again.

When it came to my turn, I used the stick too timidly: the aircraft wobbled through the air on the point of the stall until Wreford lost his patience. His voice came sharply through the slow beat of the engine and the soughing of the wind. "Bring the stick back, for heaven's sake! Get the speed right down . . ."

It seemed an unmannerly way to treat an aeroplane, but I set my teeth and hauled the stick into my lap. "That's better," said Wreford, as the kaleidoscope of fields and woodland swung up ahead. "Stick forward now, and recover — keep her straight with rudder. Regain your height and we'll try one more for luck."

The technique for landing was rather similar. The difference was that there was no 4,000 feet to play with if you got it wrong. The trick was to hold off, as close the the ground as your judgement would allow, until that point before the stall when the aircraft began to sink. When you sensed that moment had arrived, you pulled the stick right back, and let the aircraft settle. Ideally, the wings would let the wheels take the weight at the place on the grass where you wanted to touch down. But hold off too high, and you would pass beyond the sinking stage to the nose-dropping stage: the wheels would hit first, the aircraft would bounce, stall again, bounce again, and move across the airfield like a tiring kangaroo: too low, before the flying speed was lost, and you would be back in the air again like a kangaroo rejuvenated. To make a good landing — a proper three-point landing, that is, with the wheels and the tail-skid touching down together — the speed, height and attitude had to be right. It was a very satisfying thing to do — like bowling on a length and hitting middle stump.

For the first time in my life, a birthday went unmarked by gifts or kisses, or by twenty candles on a cake: birthdays were for home, not for the Air Force. Nor did the Japanese attack, that day, on Hawaii and the Philippines mean more to us at Ansty, isolated in our world of lift, drag, weight and thrust, than the thought that, if we were sent to America for training, it would be as Allies in uniform, not pretending to be civilians in a neutral country, as those on the early courses on The Arnold Scheme had done. This struck us as good news, since most of us had only been in uniform for a month or so, and were still enjoying the thrill and the pride of it.

39

What we didn't know (and there were such a lot of things the future held that we were unaware of) was that the US Army Air Corps looked on its trainees as officer cadets, and that was all right if you wore a sports jacket and flannels as those on the first few courses did — that way you were welcome to the club — but, since the RAF only saw fit to make us LACs, our rank would not entitle us to breathe the same air as American cadets. To them, the little badges on our sleeves could merely mean that we were cleared to swing a prop, or prime an engine — tasks for the lowliest Joe on the flight line.

But all that lay ahead: what we knew for the moment was that we were standing on the threshold of achievement — solo flight. Just two exercises were to be completed before that moment came: "Powered approach and landing" and "Spinning", and I was looking forward more to the one than to the other. It stood to reason that approaching under power would be a lot easier than with the propeller windmilling — if your cross-wind turn had been a little late, you could use the engine to make up the deficit — but to put an aeroplane so out of control that it helplessly spun about its vertical axis seemed to be an even grosser act than stalling. Nevertheless, it had to be done — not only done, but thoroughly mastered. "You can get into a spin by accident," said Wreford. "It can happen any time. You've got to be able to get out of it."

"Yes, sir."

"It's good fun, actually. You'll enjoy it."

40

Then came the fog, day after day in mid-December. We stayed huddled in the flight hut, glad of the Sidcot suits, writing with our fingers on the misted windows. "Even the wee birds are walking," muttered Walker, lighting half a cigarette. We wrote letters home, told jokes, played pontoon, shared hopes of flying the fighter or the bomber of our choice and made guesses about where we might be posted next. We did our share of the routine station chores, and one of these — the guard — inspired an anecdote which was only remarkable for not being based on some sexual aberration. It was McLeod, lounging near the coke-fire, cap slanted rakishly across his glossy head, who told the tale. "It's about two in the morning," he said, "and the Orderly Officer's fast asleep in his bed when the phone rings. It's the Orderly Sergeant. 'Sorry to bother you, Sir, but there's been a bit of trouble at No 2 Gate.' The OO says what does he mean — trouble? 'It's the sentry, Sir. He's shot a man.' 'Shot a man, Sergeant? Is he badly hurt?' 'No, Sir, more what you might call dead.' 'Are you trying to tell me, Sergeant, that the sentry at No 2 Gate has killed a man?' 'That's it, Sir.' 'Why on earth did he do that?' 'Dunno, Sir.'"

McLeod did the voices well, if with an element of caricature. His officer voice was clearly modelled on Ralph Lynn, the "silly ass of Ben Travers' farces, and his Sergeant was reminiscent of Bill the Bastard. He had our attention, so far, by this device.

"The OO gets dressed in a hurry," McLeod continued, "and trots along to No 2 Gate. They haul the sentry in front of him. 'What's your name, airman?'

41

the OO asks. 'Snodgrass 468, Sir.' 'I'm told you've had a bit of an accident, Snodgrass.' 'It wasn't no accident, Sir.'"

McLeod's sentry had a high-pitched Cockney accent and a slight stammer. "'You'd better tell me exactly what happened,' says the OO, 'in your own words. Take your time.' 'Well, Sir, it was like this. I was detailed for duty on No 2 Gate from twenty-three fifty-nine hours till oh-three fifty-nine. I reported to my place of duty at . . .' The OO told him not to take his time to quite that extent, and get to the point."

Garrett lay back in a chair and yawned. "I know how he felt."

McLeod ignored the interruption. "'At approximately oh-one forty-five hours, I detected the sound of individuals approaching my post, Sir, so I give the challenge — "'Alt," I says, "'oo goes there." "Friend," says an individual, "'an" I thought, 'ello, that's funny, an' I says, "Advance one, an' give the password." That's when me suspicions was confirmed, Sir.' 'What do you mean, man?' 'Well, Sir, this individual says, "Yellow Duster", Sir. So I shot 'im.'"

McLeod paused briefly to flick a speck of ash from his sleeve. "The OO jumps up and smacks the old forehead. 'But for goodness sake, Snodgrass, "Yellow Duster" *is* the password'! 'Oh, yes, Sir,' says Snodgrass, 'but our chaps always say "Shove off".'"

I didn't spin the Tiger Moth and I didn't fly it solo — none of us did. Before the fog had cleared, we were sent on embarkation leave, with orders to report at Heaton

Park in Manchester on Boxing Day. Struggling with both kitbags on Harrow Station platform, I was greeted by my mother's choice of taxi-driver, the venerable Mr Phillips, and by one of a group of girls in khaki who were also alighting from the London train. Recognition wasn't instant: the stunning figure was shapeless in the uniform, the Christmas doll face was ablaze with rouge and lipstick, and the fine-spun hair was set in waves so permanent as to appear, not only indestructible, but untouchable.

"Hello, Marie," I said, adding perceptively, "I see you've joined the ATS."

"All the nice boys are in the Forces now — what was a girl to do?"

Thankfully, I let Mr Phillips take a kitbag. "Can I give you a lift, Marie?"

"Daddy's meeting me, thanks." She nodded towards her companions, who were conversing among themselves in a chorus of squeals. "I'm taking some of the gang home for the hols."

"Merry Christmas."

"Same to you. Remember we've got a date to catch up on — I'll give you a ring. See you later, alligator."

"In a while, crocodile."

That night, crawling from pub to club to pub, I worked my way back into the Harrow atmosphere and listened to the news. Marie was right: most of my contemporaries, nice or not, were in the Services, but there were enough on leave, medically unfit or working on something "of national importance" to make a small social whirl. The word was that, among the girls, Sandy was known to be saving her kisses for me. Others, though by no means out of reach, had been more liberal with their favours. Hermione, indeed, had gone so far as to marry a soldier, which put her out of bounds for what I had in mind.

"Sandy," I said, walking her home from the Embassy cinema next night, "will you let me sleep with you before I go back?"

She giggled, and nudged me sharply in the ribs. "Gosh, what a thing to come out with! You do say some awful things."

"What's awful about it? I think it would be jolly nice."

"I don't know about nice, but it's — well, it's wrong, isn't it?"

"Who says it's wrong," I apostatised, "if we want to?"

"I don't know — people. Mum, anyway." She walked on in silence for a while, occasionally squeezing my hand. She was tall enough to match her stride with mine. Then she stopped and put her hands on my shoulders. Her fair cap of curls shone dully in the darkness, her strong, small face was a sweet-smelling shadow. "Why do you want to?"

I hesitated. "Because I want to find out what it's like" wouldn't do. I took a deep breath and licked my lips. "Because I love you," I said, and felt the heavy strangeness of the words — like those of the oath I'd sworn at Weston, "and I want to make love to you, properly. Don't you want to?"

She stood for a moment, looking into my eyes, before we walked on, side by side, not touching. "Have you done it before," she asked. "I mean, have you slept with anyone else?"

"Of course not."

A late bus crunched slowly by towards North Harrow, its shrouded headlights painting a streak of brightness on the road. "Betty slept with John," I wheedled, "before he went to sea." I knew that Sandy took a good view of Betty, for her ladylike air and her skill at table-tennis. I could have added that Betty slept with Ted, Doug and Alec, but that would not have helped the cause.

"How do you know?"

"I just know — everybody knows."

She tossed her head. "That doesn't make it right."

"You're so old-fashioned. I bet all the chaps in my Flight are doing it with their sweethearts — probably at this very moment."

She giggled again, and put her arm around my waist. "Serve them right if they all have babies."

"You wouldn't have a baby. I can take precautions."

"You know a lot about it, don't you?"

"I've heard other chaps talking. I know what they do."

She sang a tune, softly, as we walked — one I'd often sung to her: "There is nothing for me but to love you, just the way you look tonight . . ." Then she said, "You've never asked me to marry you, or get engaged or anything."

"Sandy," I reproved her, "I'm going overseas after Christmas, perhaps for a year, perhaps for ever, I don't know. A chap doesn't go around getting engaged to people if he might never see them again."

She was considering this piece of sophistry when a high-flying aircraft throbbed across North Harrow, heading east. It might have been on a peaceful mission — a communication flight or a cross-country exercise — but it probably turned Sandy's thoughts to my uncertain future, for when we kissed goodnight at her gate, she whispered, "Mum's taking Auntie Doris her Christmas presents on Thursday. She'll be out all afternoon."

Whoever that lone pilot was up there, I wished him fair weather and very happy landings.

CHAPTER
FOUR

The Cold Atlantic and the Stratford Seven

The first day at Heaton Park Aircrew Holding Centre was spent at one counter or another of the vast clothing store, cramming what kitbag space remained with the sort of clothing you would need to pass your winters in the Arctic and your summers in the tropics. Blind authority, it seemed, either didn't know where we were going or didn't care if we humped and dumped these multi-purpose wardrobes there and back — never needing more than would have occupied a suitcase.

That evening, in a news theatre (the seats were cheaper there than in a proper cinema, and Christmas had pauperised most of us) we were cheered by the pictures of British tanks advancing through the Libyan desert and of German tanks being less successful on the way to Moscow.

At our billet in a dark suburb of Manchester, the landlady served steaming plates of hotpot. Hovering round the table, adjusting here a glass of water, there a cruet, Mrs Wood advised us to abandon any thought we might have had of seeking entertainment in the arms of local lasses. "I don't want you doing anything as your own mothers wouldn't be pleased for you to do, not while you're in my house, I don't."

"My Mam doesna mind me going oot wi' girls," protested Walker.

"Mine encourages it," McLeod agreed. "Have you any daughters, Mrs Wood?"

"I'd never forgive myself," continued our adviser. "I'd never be able to look your mothers in the face. Now, I've got a lovely roly-poly pudding for your afters, and then you can come in and listen to the wireless with Mr Wood and me before you go to bed like good lads."

When, next day, we were obliged to watch yet another film about the horrors of VD, it seemed that all of Manchester was conspiring to enforce a celibate regime. It was only a surviving spirit of defiance that led Withers, Burt and me to Sefton's Saturday dance. Flush with a week's pay of two pounds, ten shillings in our pockets, it was the work of but a moment to engage the attention of three pretty WAAFs. But the memory of those horrible afflictions, and of their more unpleasant treatment, must have had an impact, for we confined our intercourse to chatter, and I felt distinctly reckless when I kissed my share of the trio a perfunctory goodnight.

On Sunday morning, 4th January, the draft was assembled in one of those great cinemas that had been beyond our means, to be addressed by an officer whose rank was even further out of reach. As he spoke, I marvelled at the rungs on the ladder — Corporal,

Sergeant, Flight Sergeant, Warrant Officer, Pilot Officer, Flying Officer, Flight Lieutenant, Squadron Leader, Wing Commander, Group Captain — that lay between our station and the giddy heights of his. It seemed improbable that we could share a common language, and yet, if you shut your eyes to the thick tapes on his sleeves and the gold braid on his cap, he was no deity, merely a mortal man — no orator, either, but searching for words, pleasantly avuncular, and far less frightening than Corporal Bill had been.

We were soon to be posted, the Air Commodore told us, to the USA and in this we were fortunate young men: the training there would be of the highest order, in unparalleled conditions of environment and climate, far away from blackouts, bombs and rationing; this good fortune, however, carried its responsibilities, for every man would be looked on as an ambassador of Britain in a foreign land — a land long our friend and now our ally. Customs and traditions there were different from our own, and some of us might find the way of life a little strange; we would do well to bear in mind the maxim "When in Rome, live as the Romans do", and keep our own counsel at times when differences of opinion or behaviour might arise.

There was more in this vein from which my attention drifted, as it tended to do when anybody sought to tell me how I should behave, but the Air Commodore regained it when he turned to the matter of security. This, he said, required that our destination must as yet remain a secret to the outside world: our journey would be imperilled by anyone who talked of it — even to a

49

parent, a sweetheart or a wife. Neither the post nor the telephone could be regarded as secure, so we must "keep mum", in the words of the poster, and only when we reached our destination could we send a cable home to tell our next-of-kin of our arrival.

Forewarned of this constraint and having learned from all the spy stories that a random, one-time code was impossible to break, I had arranged a simple cypher: a mention of pears in a letter home would indicate Rhodesia, apples would mean Canada and oranges America. Two days later, sitting on the deck of HMT *Wolfe*, as she lay at anchor in the gently rocking waters of the Clyde, I wrote ". . . and through the morning mist, the sun looks like an orange."

The draft had assembled on the previous evening, and marched through the silent streets to Prestwich, where the hours until the train was due were passed in the Co-op hall and a state of suppressed excitement, relieved at midnight by an impromptu and increasingly bawdy concert for which I had detailed to act as the MC.

"Right, son," the RTO Sergeant had eventually said, "we're moving on. Tell 'em to form up outside in ten minutes."

"One last song before we go, gentlemen," I had boomed through the microphone. "What's it to be — 'Jerusalem', 'Land of Hope and Glory' or 'God Save the King'?"

"No," they had roared, "Eff 'em all!" Well, I had done my best.

"Eff 'em all, eff 'em all,
The long and the short and the tall;
Eff all the Sergeants and Double-you Oh Ones,
Eff all the Corporals and their bastard sons;
'Cause we're saying goodbye to them all,
As back to their billets they crawl —
They'll get no promotion this side of the ocean,
So cheer up my lads, eff 'em all!"

On the journey north, the train had paused in Carlisle, where the blessed WVS provided steaming mugs of tea, and steamed on to Gourock through Motherwell and Glasgow, where Walker had pressed his button nose against the window and, for once, fallen silent.

The tender had carried us in relays to the troopship, moving with a gentle, rocking motion, which had been sufficient to induce among a few a mal-de-mer, and that hadn't augured well for their enjoyment of the coming voyage. The tender took my coded letter in the mail-bag to port — a contact with land that was to be the last for fourteen days.

The Stratford group's accommodation was not the most salubrious to be found aboard the ship: it was on the mess-deck, next to the galley, way back astern and just above the Plimsoll line. A cheery seaman showed us how to sling the hammocks and, as cheerily, charged half-a-crown for the two bits of wood that held the ends apart. The resulting contraption didn't look comfortable, but it was — once you had mastered the knack of getting into it without doing a barrel roll. That night, I slept like a dead man, while the ship stood silent on the softly-lapping tide.

Next day, at noon, the *Wolfe* moved out into the Firth of Clyde and steamed slowly south between the Isle of Arran and the Ayrshire coast. "In the canteen," said Featonby, appearing at the deck-rail, "there's as many cigarettes and chocolates as you want — it's just like peacetime." The coastline faded, the breeze began to penetrate our greatcoats, and we went below to play pontoon until the call for "lights out". Fully dressed, and wearing a life-jacket (ship's orders were insistent about that), I slept again like a body embalmed. It seemed like a moment before the clatter of cutlery and the smell of bacon frying announced another day, and it took no longer to swing out of the hammock and take a place at table.

To breakfast so, unshaven and unwashed, seemed decidedly raffish, if not downright degenerate — I wouldn't have got away with it at home — but so limited were the facilities on HMT *Wolfe* that anyone attempting their ablutions at that hour of the day did so at the risk of missing breakfast altogether. Featonby, predictably, contrived to rise early, and was as neat as Whitehall must have seen him at his best. For the rest, apart from the grizzled Garrett, and Jimmy Withers, who had an innate ability to appear unkempt at any time, two or three days without a razor didn't make much difference to our chins.

When the morning lifeboat drill was held, the ship was steaming southward in the Irish Sea; she passed St David's Head in the early afternoon and came to anchor in Milford Haven, among the mastheads that stood stark above the surface of the sound. "It's a ships' graveyard," said Lawton with a shudder. "I hope we don't stay here long."

"They've been sunk on purpose, mate," said Burt. "Block-ships, they are, to stop the old U-boats sneaking in."

"Oh, yes? And what do you know about it? Get a lot of shipping round the Clapham Common area, do you, Percy?"

"It's in the blood, mate — sea-faring nation and all that." He glanced westward, down the sound, shading his eyes with a seamanly hand. "The convoy'll form up here, I reckon. Well, stands to reason, doesn't it? Last port of call before the old Atlantic. Safety in numbers, mate, against the bloody U-boats — and the *Tirpitz*."

We stared at this new, nautically knowledgeable Burt. "*Tirpitz*?"

"Your Jerry pocket battleship — Christ, don't you know anything about the war at sea?"

"Actually," said Featonby, "the *Tirpitz* is bottled up in the Baltic. It daren't come out."

"Don't you believe it, Ron. It might bust out any minute and come belting across the old Atlantic, looking for such as us. That's why we'll sail in a great convoy, see?"

This forecast of a great marshalling of British sea-power to our side proved optimistic: when the convoy formed, even Burt had to admit that a solitary frigate and another tatty troopship fell short of what he had in mind. Nevertheless, it was in this company that the *Wolfe* set course that afternoon. By next morning, she was in the North Atlantic and rolling on those greenies like an empty barrel. Johnson had been one of those most affected by the motion of the tender as it crossed the gentle Clyde; now, he was quite brought down, and sat throughout the day, with others equally distressed, swathed in blankets on the windswept after-deck, his long, comedian's face a greenish-yellow shade. Mustering for lifeboat drill, we called a hearty greeting, and he responded with the sickliest of grins.

That afternoon, in what had been the first-class dining room before the *Wolfe* became a troopship, as many of the draft as could be crowded in were treated to a talk by a famous fighter-pilot who, on a rest from operations, was bound for a lecture tour in the USA. Squadron Leader Gwilliam was physically slight, with fair, wavy hair a little longer than the norm and a youthful appearance, except for the network of lines around his eyes. He wore his tunic with the top button unfastened, in the fighter-pilot's fashion, a row of ribbons and a pair of tennis shoes, for which he apologised — he had left a burning Spitfire just too late to save his toes. His talk, from what I heard of it (he spoke very quietly) was about the way the US Army Air Corps trained their pilots. I must have been only one of many who would have liked to have heard a word about his combat experience but, such were the inhibitions of the day, the obligatory reticence, which made the slightest hint of "line-shooting" utterly taboo, that no one asked the hero to say a word about himself.

Later in the voyage, when he passed the Stratford Seven's table on one of his visits to the lower deck, I took my chance. "I'm going to fly bombers, Sir," I said, and added as my class-mates guffawed, "Well, that's the intention . . ."

The Squadron Leader perched himself, cross-legged, on the table and gave an encouraging smile.

"I was wondering if you could tell us how not to get shot down by a fighter?"

He was silent for a moment, straightening the creases of his trousers at the knees, and I realised that, since his Spitfire was unlikely to have ignited by spontaneous combustion, the question might have been rather tactless, but he accepted a cigarette from Skinner and looked me in the eye. "Don't let him get a good shot at you," he said, so quietly that we all leaned forward to catch the words through the throb of the turbines. "Deflection shots are difficult, and the bigger the deflection, the more difficult they are."

He used his hands to illustrate the point: left hand for the bomber, right for the fighter, approaching dead astern. "Piece of cake, no deflection." He turned the bomber hand away, and the fighter hand followed, but turning more steeply. "Not so easy. Now he's having to aim at where he thinks you're going to be."

People were rising from their seats and moving nearer, but he didn't seem to notice. His bomber hand made a climbing turn to port, then a diving turn to starboard. "Now it's getting difficult. He can't get a good shot in if you jink around like that."

"Meanwhile," I suggested, "my rear gunner . . ."

He smiled, turned the fighter hand steeply, made the sound of gunfire by blowing through his lips and let the other hand fall. "Keen on bombers?"

"Yes, Sir."

He glanced round at his audience. "I must be going. No, don't get up." He rose, hands in his pockets, and looked down at me. "Good luck, Butch!" He walked away, carefully, between the dining tables, leaving me with counsel I would always remember, and with a nickname that the Stratford Seven would never allow me to forget.

In the afternoon of 10th January, Burt announced that a gale was blowing up. The *Wolfe* must have heard him, because she started to behave rather more eccentrically, adding pitching and tossing to the rolling and yawing we had come to know if not to love. Her path through the water resembled that of a corkscrew, and the group of the unwell on the after-deck swelled by the minute. Withers, wearing a balaclava helmet that made his head look like a turnip in a badly-holed sock, brought news of our sister-ship. "Apparently," he said, "the electric steering gear's broken down. They've got eight men at the wheel and they still can't hold her on course."

"Just a minute," said Burt, jealous of his status as our nautical adviser, "where did you get all this gen from?"

"I got friends in high places on this vessel, mate. They keep me informed."

The prow climbed high into the lurid sky, with foam-flecked fountains spraying the decks, paused as though uncertain of the way to go, swerved and plunged into a trough between two tall ridges in the roaring seascape. That night, swinging in the hammock, I heard sounds from the galley of the breaking of crockery, the clanging of pots and the sliding of pans — as though a gang of poltergeists were holding a convention. Breakfast next morning wasn't up to par, but the cooks produced a Sunday lunch — turkey and Christmas pudding — of which my mother would have approved. The sound of the gale and the tang of the spray were appetite-enhancing, and I approached every meal with a keenness only briefly blunted when an ill-fitting porthole cover allowed a stream of salty water to splash across the table.

On Monday, although the *Wolfe*'s speed had been reduced to help her to keep station, our sister-ship was nowhere to be seen. She was somewhere far astern — and the frigate with her. McLeod scanned the horizon, over which was sweeping a sudden sheet of snow. "This is jolly good," he said, "all alone in the middle of the ocean. Where's the Navy gone?"

"There's probably a U-boat lining us up this very minute," growled Garrett. "Honest — wherever I look, I can see a periscope."

"It's no joke," said Withers, "this area's absolutely thick with the bastards."

Featonby sniffed. "How on earth do you know? You haven't the faintest idea where we are."

"I've been working it out, mate, and we're bang in the middle of their killing ground." Excitedly, he pointed at the heaving grayness on the starboard beam.

"Look there, for Christ's sake! Isn't that a torpedo, coming straight at us?"

Walker cast a quick glance to the right. "Shut your head, you panicky wee bugger," he said, "or I'll throw you overboard. I'm away below for a game of pontoon."

We played the game by the hour for a penny a card. Charlie Davison, the eighth man at the table, ran out of pennies and issued IOUs in all directions; he owed me ninety pounds, but Featonby advised that the debt could not be legally pursued, and I had lost the evidence, anyway.

The talk that afternoon was from a ferry-pilot, who flew various types of aircraft from the factories of Martin and Consolidated Aircraft, in the USA, to airfields in Britain. He wore a leather flying-jacket, a crumpled peaked cap on the back of his head, and talked of transatlantic navigation in an easy, pleasant way but, although he flew a lot of bombers, he was not, for me, a bomber-pilot, and no question came to mind when he offered us the chance.

Ship's duties for the draft comprised fatigues, security guard and crewing the Bofors gun — the *Wolfe*'s only armament. There were so many of us to share out the duties that the chances were against being on the roster more than once. When my turn came around, it was for fatigues — humping barrels in the canteen — which wasn't quite so boring as guarding nameless stores against an unknown predator, and a lot less chilling than manning the gun. Withers and I, co-humpers, heard the rhythmic pounding — like a pneumatic drill working in slow-time — as the gunners fired their practice rounds out there in the cold, and agreed that fatigues were not too bad at all.

The next day, the weather was so hostile — "she's shipping the greenies," Burt remarked — that only the gun-crew were allowed on deck. Down below, the Purser changed our sterling into dollars. "I don't call this money," said McLeod, fingering a note, "we play Monopoly with stuff like this at home."

Walker thumbed his roll, and went into his W. C. Fields routine: "Five, ten, fifteen, sixteen . . . how did that wee one get in there?" He peeled off the dollar bill and tossed it away. "Twenty, twenty-five . . ." Lawton bent quickly to salvage the reject, but Walker's foot was quicker.

With nightfall came the sound of heavy gunfire, booming in the distance to the north. No one told us what it meant — perhaps nobody knew — and it had been forgotten by the time the craggy coast of Nova Scotia appeared on the horizon with the dawn. The *Wolfe* dropped her anchor in Halifax harbour after fourteen days at sea, in the stinging cold of the late afternoon, the brilliance of which faded into twilight as we prepared to disembark.

There was a moment, standing on deck with collar buttoned up and hands deep in pockets, while the shore-lights shone serenely and shimmered on the water, when it truly reached me that embattled, blacked-out Britain was 2,000 miles away, and that beyond the starlit harbour lay another world. I shuffled down the gangway, with Walker ahead of me, Featonby behind. On the far side of the snow-covered pier, hissing patiently, stood the train that was to take the draft to Moncton in New Brunswick. I stepped across the threshold into North America, slipped on a patch of ice, and landed on my back.

CHAPTER
FIVE

The Old Bush Pilot

The next three days were marked by sudden change and new experience: the sleep-inducing rumble of the Moncton train as it journeyed through the night; the slipping, stumbling, kitbag-laden trek across two miles of ice; the sizzling breakfast and the dry warmth of the wooden barrack-huts; the frozen streets where stocky children, wearing fur-lined caps and lumber-jackets, ran after us to beg for British coins; the awesome pyrotechnics of the Aurora Borealis; the taxi-drivers who could always find a way around the liquor laws; the accent of the people — almost the American we knew from Hollywood, but with a more familiar sound, as though a European heritage was remembered in the tongue.

On 22nd January 1942, reveille was at 4a.m. for a return to the station — or depot, as the RCAF called it — and the southbound train. We crossed the border, still in darkness, switched trains in Maine and travelled on in greater comfort, cosseted by stewards, through the states of New England, gazing at the place-names as they flashed by the windows — Boston, Providence, Bridgeport and Yonkers.

Determined to tread the streets of New York, however brief the stop, I ran along the platform of Pennsylvania Station, out into the empty brightness of the city at seven in the morning, and halted in a doorway. "Milk-shake, buddy?" asked the young man at the counter. "Chocolate, orange, lemon . . ."

"Just a glass of milk, please."

"Plain milk, buddy?"

"If you have such a thing."

"Sure, I do. Hey, you're English, right?"

I drank the milk in two gulps and asked the cost. "Forget it, old bean," the young man drawled, in a brave attempt at a Mayfair accent. "On the jolly old house."

"Thanks very much."

"You're welcome."

"I have to catch a train — cheerio."

"Toodle-pip!"

Featonby was standing at the carriage door. "Where the blazes have you been?" he asked crossly. "You nearly got left behind."

"I like it here, Ron. Chuck my kitbags out, will you — I think I'll stay."

"Get in, you silly sod." As the train rolled on through New Jersey, he settled down austerely to read the *New York Times*, and I to write a letter home. Withers, Burt and Lawton were engrossed in movie magazines; McLeod and Walker slept, while Johnson, with the ocean but a memory, was building up his strength by means of Hershey bars.

"Washington DC, gen'lemen, capital city of the United States," crooned a steward, and pointed out the landmarks: Grant's Tomb, the Senate building, the National Shrine. Neither he nor we could be aware that, not a mile away, a certain RAF Air Marshal — one Arthur T. Harris — having completed a mission to the USA, was packing his bags for the journey home; there were, however, many in that carriage who would know more of that Air Marshal in the years to come.

The train moved on southward, through the woodlands of Virginia and the Carolinas, along the Piedmont fall-line below the Appalachians and, early in the morning of 24th January, at last into Atlanta. From that hub of Georgia's life, a fleet of Greyhound coaches took us on across the plains beside the winding River Flint to Turner Field.

Those who stepped out of the coaches into the brightness of the morning were a fraction only of the host of pale, young men who, like chickens in a battery-house, had thronged the troopship *Wolfe*. Some had gone to RAF-run courses in the BFTS Scheme, which had schools in Texas, Arizona, Florida and California, some to train as Navy fliers on the coast of Florida in the Towers Scheme, while we at Turner Field were to be Class 42H within the US Army Air Corps training system — The Arnold Scheme — and, although our progress would be monitored by the RAF, we would in all essentials be treated like American cadets. We would be taught to fly their aircraft by their flying instructors, be subject to their discipline and wear their uniform — except for two items of our own

63

— we kept the tie and forage-cap (McLeod was glad of that). If, having passed through every phase of the training, and measured up to USAAC standards, we would be rewarded with their flying badge — the silver wings that gleamed upon the tunic of the officer who greeted us, and was to be our Flight Commander for the month at Turner Field.

The facilities of the base were impressive, the barracks comfortable and the food magnificent. A cheerful retinue of coloured men waited at table (I was beginning to wonder whether any white American ever served himself) and, although the day of our arrival was locally judged to be among the coldest of the year, to me it seemed like summer.

The trouble with Turner was that it had no aeroplanes for us: what it had was a course of "Orientation" — not, in 1942, a word in common British use. Skinner thought that it meant being concerned about the East and, as all America was currently vexed about the Japanese, that seemed to make some sense. It turned out, however, to have nothing to do with that: it had to do with what the Air Commodore had spoken of at Heaton Park — of living, when in Rome, the way the Romans did.

As the story came out later, experience had shown that those on early British courses on The Arnold Scheme, going direct to flying schools, had met so many problems in adjusting to the USAAC ethic in general and to USAAC discipline in particular — the West Point style was characterised by its critics as combining the least attractive aspects of a Prussian

military academy and an English boarding school —
that their progress had been seriously impaired.
Misunderstandings had arisen, leading to resentment,
even to acrimony and, once or twice, so it was said, to
open mutiny.

Close by the Guardroom of any RAF Station, you
would find a little building labelled "ET Room" ("ET"
for "early treatment"). There, if you had recently been
familiar with a rather careless girl, you could take
prophylactic measures before it was too late. To provide
such measures against the anti-Roman syndrome
appeared to be the role of Turner Field and, in this
regard, our Flight Commander had been well chosen
for the task. To see First Lieutenant Honnicutt's
deeply-tanned, good-humoured face and hear his
warm, Southern accent was to feel that not much could
be wrong with any Service of which he was an officer.

Certainly, he was different: there can't have been
many British Flight Commanders who welcomed the
latest draft by crooning the latest hit-song in the base
cinema, and even fewer who, on short acquaintance,
imparted the details of a happy married life, and
produced a pretty, smiling wife to illustrate his point.
Different, yes, but totally disarming and obviously
decent.

The drill was different, too. On parade at Turner
Field, men didn't turn, they faced — "left face, right
face, about face" — and "about face" was a whole new
exercise, reversing the movement taught by Bill the
Bastard of a pivot on the right foot and a pickup with
the left. There was some teetering and tottering before

we got the knack. We soon became accustomed to "Tay — hut" for "Ah — ten — shun", and to "Hup, two three" for "Left, right, left", and it was relatively easy — even pleasant — to adapt our stiff-armed, straight-backed way of marching to the more relaxed style of the Army Air Corps. One thing we weren't required to imitate was the Air Corps flat-handed, flick-away salute: we stuck to Stratford teaching — longest way up, shortest way down, with the palm to the front and the tip of the index finger touching the temple.

The Orientation process took up a large slice of the day, beginning at six in the darkness of the morning with half-an-hour's PT — none the less dire for being called "Callisthenics" — and continuing till lessons ended at six-thirty in the evening, with further seemingly informal but well-planned contacts out of duty hours.

Corporal Bill, at his most bastardly, couldn't have asked for more marching than we did, on duty and off. If, when Featonby and I visited the Post Exchange — an up-market version of the NAAFI — or I accompanied McLeod to post a letter, we failed to march in step, side-by-side, making "square turns" at every corner, some sharp-eyed NCO would appear from nowhere with a reprimand.

So, on parade and in the barrack-blocks, in the classrooms and the mess-hall, the PX and the cinema, the Lieutenant and his sergeants did their best to "orient" Class 42H to the life-style of America. From them, I gained a series of impressions — some favourable, some not so — that would remain in my mind, as first impressions will, right or wrong, for life. There was the unquestioning and mutual acceptance of the colour-bar, the necessity to be a "regular guy", the adulation of "mom" and small children, the dread of cynicism, the belief that nonconformity was a social evil, the moral need to own a monster motor-car, and the tendency to equate religious faith with patriotism, as though God and Uncle Sam were really one.

We moved about a lot in double-time at Turner Field, and there was absolutely no escape from daily callisthenics. What with this and all the protein in the diet, it was impossible to avoid becoming physically fit. A skinny five-foot-nine on leaving ACRC, I grew two inches more and tipped the scales at ten-stone-ten. Muscles were appearing where skin and bone had been before, and this was just as well, for hostile strangers, hearing of my nickname and unaware of how unapt it was, sometimes required a demonstration of its worth. It was only thanks to Garrett that I didn't come to harm. He taught me how to guard myself, how to punch my weight — such as it was — and how to get in close when things got out of hand. As Dickens' Fagin taught his protégés a certain sleight of hand, so Garrett revealed a dirty trick or two, for use in an emergency. Although, so armed, I didn't need to shrink from little combats, I never sought one, and much preferred a gentler sort of sport.

We played volley-ball and softball, ran obstacle and relay races, and strove at tug-of-war. At one session on the sports field, the instructors produced a wicker hamper and stood aside, beaming, while we, like children with a Christmas gift, unpacked a set of cricket stumps, two hockey balls, assorted pads and gloves, two bats and a score-book. That the bats were only schoolboy size was not important, but having never seen a drop of oil, they looked so palely brittle in the glaring sun that the cricketers among us couldn't bear to use them. "One ball on the edge of one of those," said Skinner, "and it'll splinter. Linseed oil is what they need." The Sergeant rubbed the stubble of his crew-cut. "Linseed oil, huh? I don't believe we . . . say, we do have a lubricant — an automobile lubricant. How'd that be?"

"Not quite the same thing, Sergeant, wouldn't do at all."

He looked so disappointed that we played a sort of cricket, using a pair of softball bats. He and his Corporals joined in with spirit, yelping like foxhounds and hurling the ball from the outfield like a rocket, directly at the bowler. When the Sergeant was persuaded to take a turn at the wicket, he ignored any delivery other than a comfortable full-toss and, having made contact, at once dropped the bat and made off smartly towards cover-point. Nevertheless, it made a pleasant change from drill and guard duty, from lectures on the history of the USAAC, the State of Georgia, Continental engines, hygiene, "Military Courtesy", weaponry and climate. Most of all, it was a break from indoctrination in the "Honour System" — a code of conduct which required that, in any breach of regulations, you informed, not only on your classmates, but on yourself, and that they, in turn, informed on you.

After a fortnight, when the course at Turner Field was half-way through, "Open Post" was granted every other evening; we had to be back on the base and bedded down by "Lights Out" at ten. This gave just enough time to take the four-mile bus-ride into Albany (whites in the front seats, blacks in the back), go to the movies and grab a snack at Lane's Restaurant. There, in each booth, was a slave for the juke-box: you put a nickel in the slot and chose a tune from the "top twenty" to go with the meal. The Artie Shaw version of Hoagy Carmichael's "Stardust", and "A Whistler's Mother-in-Law" sung by Bing, were numbers one and two; it was number three — an up-tempo dirge called "Somebody Else Is Taking My Place" — which seemed unpleasantly apt when a Wing Commander Hogan of the RAF, visiting the base, made it clear that somebody else might well be taking our places on The Arnold Scheme. Less than half our number, revealed the Wing Commander, were likely to complete the flying training courses. There were three of these: Primary, Basic and Advanced, each of two months' duration, and the fact that there were six Primary Schools and only two Basic argued that someone had to go. But, never mind, the Wing Commander said, those who failed to make the grade in The Arnold Scheme had every chance of qualifying in Canada as some other sort of aircrew — observer or bomb-aimer.

We heard him out in silence but, on returning to the classroom, there was some muttering among the ranks.

There had been rumours already of how one cadet had been "washed out" because the folds in his blankets were a little out of line, another for failing to salute a distant officer, and yet another for not answering quickly to an upper classman's order. That was another thing we learned about at Turner Field — the class system, under which we might expect to suffer at Basic (if we should ever get so far) and Advanced. There, it appeared, two courses ran concurrently, one a month behind the other, and the senior — the "Upper Class" — wielded many minor disciplinary powers over the junior. When that class moved on, the lower took its place, with the right, and the duty, to mete out similar tyrannies in turn.

Being convinced at the time that no power on earth could come between me and that bomber cockpit, none of these forebodings worried me much. It was partly due to this misconceived sense of destiny, but rather more to a first experience of Bourbon whiskey, that I failed to attend an early callisthenics session, despite all Featonby's attempts to raise the dead.

"'Kay, Mister," said the Sergeant, "you're in trouble. You-all submit a written report, in writing, to the Lootenant at first call tomorrow, you hear?"

Compiling a letter in the stipulated format, I explained that 9th February happened to be the 400th anniversary of the charter given by Queen Elizabeth I to the founder of the school where I had been a humble pupil, and that the occasion had seemed to demand a celebration. My capacity for American liquor having turned out to be less than expected, I had been fighting a small battle for survival in the ablutions when I should have been enjoying a callisthenics session. The incident, greatly regretted, was unlikely to recur, as the next centenary would not fall due until AD 2042. I concluded with a reference to the British Prime Minister's connections with the school in question and, through his mother, as the Lieutenant would be aware, with the people of America.

Sophism apart, the excuse was basically unsound, as a check of the dates would have revealed, but after two suspenseful days I was told it was accepted and that, on this occasion, no disciplinary action would ensue. Praising yet again the magic name of Churchill, I went rejoicing on my way. Time was passing, every day brought flying nearer; arms drill was completed, rifles handed in, USAAC uniforms issued: shirts and slacks, of excellent quality, fine leather jackets; the shaggy bush-jackets and the baggy shorts from Heaton Park stayed crumpled in the bottoms of our kitbags.

The programme at the cinema on the base changed every other evening. On non-Open Post days, and if we were free of guard or fatigue duties, we paid our twenty cents and trooped in like zombies, with no idea of what the picture might be. There was a murmur of surprise when, following the feature film about a golden-hearted gangster by the name of "Boston Blackie", the screen showed *Target For Tonight*, and the crew of "F for Freddie" fighting their way to Germany and back through the searchlights and the flak.

Later, in the barrack-room, McLeod spat on the toe-cap of his shoe and began to brush it gently. "I liked

71

the bombing-run," he said. " 'Left, left, steady, steady
. . . bombs gone'! Super, that was. How did they get the
pictures where you were looking up at the bomb-aimer
from outside?"

"What they do," explained Johnson, "they put the
cameraman in a sort of hammock, slung under the
nose. Trouble is, he freezes to death on the way home,
but they don't mind that, because they've got the
picture . . ."

"Push off," said Withers. "They use a fixed camera,
automatic."

"Don't be so wet," Burt counselled. "All them
pictures . . ." (he tended to revert to the vernacular
with a fellow-Londoner) ". . . are taken on the ground.
It's all simulated, mate, 'cept for the shots from the kite
with all the flak coming up, and the tracer and that.
D'you still want to go on bombers, Butch?"

"No, it's put me right off. I think I'll put in for
Transport Command, or maybe Coastal."

"Please, Sir," whined McLeod, "don't send me on
another mission — I'm too young to die!"

"Did you see that big sod of a second dickey?" asked
Walker, polishing the badge of his cap on his
shirt-sleeve. "Och, I wanna have one like him. 'I say, old
boy, hold the jolly old pole while I have a wee slash
doon the back, there's a good fellah'!"

Playing the role of that second pilot was one Flying
Officer Gordon Woollatt who, eighteen months later,
was to fly his second tour of operations as a Flight
Commander with No 12 Squadron, while I, with that
same Squadron, was engaged upon my first. But that

was for the future: at Turner Field, our then Flight Commander approved an application from the Stratford Seven (which had meanwhile swelled to nine) that we should all be posted to the same Primary School. At a farewell sing-song in the cinema, the Lieutenant, ending our association the way he had begun it, gave an affecting, if irrelevant, rendition of a popular ballad called "My Sister and I", and gracefully accepted a gold-plated cigarette-case from the class. He was a pleasant man, with a fair tenor voice, a very pretty wife and, probably, more cigarette cases than any other First Lieutenant in the Army Air Corps.

Early next morning, a fleet of Trailways coaches drew up on the parade ground, and Class 42H, more or less orientated, went on its merry way.

An acquaintance with the USAAC battle-hymn had been a by-product of the Turner Field process. It was a rousing tune, with a comic-strip lyric, which, on such occasions, when singing tended to break out, made a change from "Nellie Dean", "Coming Round the Mountain" and "The Ball of Kirriemuir". On the forty-mile trip through the peanut country north of Albany, it echoed round the coach:

"Off we go, into the wild, blue yonder,
Climbing high into the sun;
Here they come, zooming to meet our thunder,
At 'em, boys, give her the gun!"

Featonby, who rarely permitted himself the levity of song, was studying a pamphlet. "Apparently it was

73

Souther Field where Colonel Lindbergh flew his first solo," he revealed.

"Who?" asked Withers.

"Lindbergh, dimwit — the first bloke to fly the Atlantic on his own. Souther is quite an historic airfield."

"Old Honnicutt," Lawton added, "reckoned it was the best Primary School in the Scheme."

"I should jolly well hope so," declared Skinner. "Only the best is good enough for us."

"Down we dive, spouting our flame from under,
Off with one hell of a roar . . ."

A signpost read "Smithville". To describe the tiny settlement as a one-horse town might have been to exaggerate, for the only living things to be seen as the coach passed slowly through were two little black boys, in dungarees and leather caps with ear-flaps, squatting by the roadside and smiling shyly as we waved.

"Actually," Featonby continued, "Souther doesn't belong to the Air Corps — it's run by a civvy firm, and the instructors are civvies, with the odd Army check pilot and a couple of RAF types."

"Good show," said Walker. "There'll maybe no be so much bull."

"We'll soon find out," said Burt. "I reckon the bull depends more on what sort of bastards the Upper Class are than who runs the place."

74

"That's right," agreed Garrett, lighting a Lucky Strike, "they can run you around day and night if they have a mind to."

The singers reached their climax:

"We'll live in fame or go down in flame,
For nothing can stop the Army Air Corps . . ."

And everyone joined in the irreverent reprise:

"Except the weather — nothing can stop the Army
Air Corps."

The first impressions of Souther Field epitomised the best and the worst of the place. The sound was the growl of a Continental engine in a PT-17, taking some member of Class 42G — the dreaded Upper Class — up into that same wild, blue yonder we had sung about; the sight was of another classman, less happily occupied. This unfortunate cadet, wearing best blue uniform, full pack, side-packs, water canteen bouncing on his hip, was marching steadily around the parade ground, making square turns at the corners and looking neither right nor left, except to salute the Stars and Stripes each time he passed the flag-staff.

"Blimey," said Withers, turning to one of the Upper Classmen who had met the coaches, "what's that geyser doing?"

"Him? Walking tours, of course."

"Beg pardon?"

"Punishment tours. You'll find out."

"Come on, mate," said Withers, with his most ingratiating grin, "give us the gen — what d'you get them for?"

"For being a naughty boy, you silly man. You get demerits for being naughty, and you're allowed four demerits a week. Every one over that, you walk a tour. Now come along, you people, get yourselves organised."

The PT-17 was climbing overhead. It was a single-engined biplane, with a fixed undercarriage and two open cockpits in tandem, like the Tiger Moth, but bigger, brighter, richer-sounding, as products of the USA were inclined to be. It had stars on the wing-tips, stripes on the tail, and paintwork that sparkled in the sun — no drab camouflage on Georgia's flying fields. Although the Army called it the PT-17, Stearman, the makers, following the national tendency to spell the way they spoke, called it the Kaydet, and that was how the Army designated us — as Aviation Cadets, with a "Kay".

The ground-crew on the field were also very different from their counterparts at Ansty: there, they had tended to be pale, wizened men in shabby greatcoats, forever beating their arms across their chests and blowing on their fingers. Here, they were big, smiling black men in bright shirts and baseball caps, who came to work in Fords and station-wagons which they left on the parking lot besides the Packards and Chevrolets of the flying instructors (the aircraftmen at Ansty were lucky if they had a rusty cycle in the stand behind the hangar).

76

Featonby, Davison, a Lancashireman called Challoner and I shared an instructor — a gentleman from Georgia by the name of Wallace Bacon Sheffield. Standing beside him, at our introduction, it struck me how fragile and insecure we seemed, compared with his massive composure. We were uncertain as to how he, a civilian, ought to be addressed. Featonby and Davison favoured "Sir"; I, "Mr Sheffield". It didn't much matter what Ginger Challoner called him, for no American as yet had understood his accent.

The first words of instruction set us straight. "Call me 'Sheff'," he said — and that was just about all he did say at that first encounter. He simply stood there, smiling, hands in the pockets of his leather jacket, and waited for us to communicate — which, like polite young Englishmen, we duly did. "Funny your name being Sheffield," I attempted. "Well, not funny, but, I mean . . . I was born in Sheffield. In England, you know."

He beamed and nodded, accepting the coincidence with equanimity.

"The Stearman looks jolly good," said Davison, getting back to business. "I expect it's nice to fly, isn't it?"

Sheffield beamed at him.

"I suppose the stalling speed's a bit higher than the Tiger Moth," offered Featonby. "But it's heavier, of course, with the bigger engine."

Slow turn, continued beam, continued silence.

"Two 'oondred 'n twenty 'orse poower," said Challoner.

Slightly puzzled beam on Challoner.

"We got a few hours in," persisted Davison, "on the old Tiger Moth, back home."

"I expect you've got hundreds of hours in, haven't you, Sir — I mean, Sheff?"

"I don't know whether you use the same take-off and landing drills here . . ."

"How long do most chaps take to go solo?"

"Will you be taking us right through Primary?"

At last the chatter petered out, and Sheffield eyed us placidly in turn while silent seconds passed. "Okay," he drawled, "we'll — ah — take ourselves — ah — kind of a look around the ship — ah — in the morning. Then we'll — ah — try the sky."

Such was his interpretation of the session set aside for "Instructor's Initial Briefing", and it turned out to be a fair example of his method. It was as though he had decided long ago that flying, like any other skill, could not be taught by talk, but by presence and example. That was his technique, and there was much to recommend it: later, when instructors did a lot of talking in the air, I often wished that they, like Wallace Bacon Sheffield, would simply demonstrate, shut up, and let me concentrate on doing things myself.

Anyone who could ride a bicycle, who didn't get upset on fairground roundabouts, and who took some pains to read the Pilot's Notes, could teach himself to fly a Primary Trainer well enough to get from A to B. He might not fly it up to Service standards, but that was where the system, and the instructor, played their part: they made sure he did.

The good instructor made you learn to do the things that you found difficult, and to do them well. If steep turns to the left came naturally to you, the instructor would have you make them to the right with equal accuracy; if you could make a lovely, steady barrel-roll, but your snap-rolls didn't always turn out quite so well, the instructor relentlessly insisted that they did; if you could touch down on a sixpence when you used a little motor, he would make you hit the spot "dead stick" — with throttle off.

Those more difficult manoeuvres might never be much fun, but what the system did, and that implacable presence in the front cockpit, was to ensure that you could make them if you had to — that you weren't afraid of them. It wasn't everyone, for instance, who really liked to put an aircraft in a spin, and yet you had to do that many times in training, so that, if the predicament should occur by misadventure, the actions for recovery would be instinctive and effective. You wouldn't, in your right mind, pull a hood across the cockpit to black out earth and sky, and try to fly by instruments alone: but, in case you ever found yourself in unexpected cloud, you had to make yourself an expert in this dark and lonely skill.

In the years to come, in black nights over Germany, I was to fly in cloud for many hours, and to bless the names of those who taught me how; and once, over Hamburg, the fact that they had taught me to recover from a spin would save the seven members of my crew from violent death.

But those proofs of the system lay in an unknown future. Halfway through March in 1942, I only knew what I'd been taught in nine hours' dual flying: take-offs and landings, climbing and gliding, stalling and spinning, rectangular courses and "S" turns over roads. It still came as a shock — or, perhaps, more as a thrill — when Wallace B. Sheffield threw off his shoulder-straps and pushed back his goggles as I taxied round the airfield for another take-off.

Then the time that passed before the Stearman stopped beside the check-point was like the moment when the bell rings for Round One, or when, in a waiting-room, you hear "The dentist will see you now", or when the umpire gives you guard and steps aside to let that tall, fast bowler come thundering towards you — something of all those, and something, too, of being the fellow with the ball.

Sheffield heaved his bulk out of the cockpit and, treading carefully upon the footsteps on the wing, moved along the fuselage until he stood beside me. I hoped it was the wash from the propeller that brought the moisture to his eyes as he put a gloved hand on my shoulder and shouted in my ear: "Okay, go ahead an' break yo' neck — see if I care."

This may have been the traditional exhortation, but it was new to me and, although for style it didn't match the words to the lads before the battle of Harfleur in *Henry V*, it made me laugh. I was still grinning when the wheels ceased to rumble and I was alone with the Stearman, the sky and what Isaac Newton had said about the law of gravity. If I was grinning then, it was a facial rictus, for I was very serious indeed. Whatever happened now was my responsibility: there were no broad, leather-coated shoulders up ahead to take the load if anything went wrong, nobody to say "Okay, I have it" if I lost control. This was what going solo meant: taking the load, and being in total charge. All right, fine. Wasn't this what I had joined the Air Force for?

There was a flight-line tale of an instructor who, with students who tended to go limp when things got in a tangle and to leave it all to him to straighten out, employed a training method of his own. He would remove his joystick, throw it overboard, clasp his hands behind his head and say: "You have control". He found this an effective stimulus until the day when, employing it with the Stearman upside-down and nothing on the clock, he saw in his mirror that the student followed suit. Crying "Hit the silk, you dummy," the instructor had released his straps and dropped out of the aircraft, whereupon the student (who had jettisoned a spare stick carried for the purpose) flew the Stearman back to base, where he explained that his instructor, whom he suspected wasn't properly strapped in, had fallen from the aircraft during a manoeuvre.

What I was in, however, was no fable: I was really flying, alone and rather cold. And much too tense. I was gripping the stick as though Sir Isaac would take over if I let it go. Furthermore, I was at 1,500 feet, still climbing straight ahead, when I should have turned left at 400 to stay within the pattern. Making myself relax, holding the stick lightly with the fingers, caressing the rudder-bar with the toes, I levelled out and made a steady left-hand turn. That was better. I looked down the line of the lower wing to check the location of the field. Field? What field? There were hundreds of them, and none of them an airfield. The cold feeling came back; it seemed to be concentrated around the lower intestine. Had anyone ever got lost on a first solo before? Apart from failing to go solo at all, there couldn't be a surer way to get a one-way railway ticket back to Moncton.

A mental picture came of Wallace Bacon Sheffield standing at the check-point, watching as his student disappeared into the distance. I remembered the way he had of asking, whenever we'd been out of the pattern for a while, "Okay, which way's the field?" You needed what my mother called a bump of direction, a cell in your brain that kept a record of how far you'd flown north, how far west and so on — that really was "Orientation", and it was what I needed now. There was only one direction in which the field could be, if I screwed down hard on the panic and thought about it calmly. I turned another ninety degrees to port by the compass, and searched the wide, pale-brown expanse of Georgia which lay below the left-hand engine cylinders. Then I remembered that the Stearman was still at 1,500 feet, and that we had always flown the pattern at 800 — which made quite a difference to the way the landscape looked. I pulled the throttle back, dropped the nose and there it was — the dry, brown expanse of the field, the white water-tower, the two big hangars and the neat row of Stearmans drawn up on the flight-line. Splendid Souther Field, good old Souther Field!

Joining the pattern in a shallow dive, I swept past another Stearman which was flying straight and level, in the orthodox way. The sun flashed on the pilot's goggles as he turned a startled head. It wasn't done to overtake another aircraft on the downwind leg, and, if an instructor had been on board, he might have been peeved enough to do something horrible, like taking the number of my aircraft and wreaking vengeance later. Happily, the startled pilot was alone. Waving an apologetic hand, I slotted in ahead of him, levelled out at 800 feet and got the airspeed back to where it should have been. After that, it was simply a matter of doing what I'd been taught: a standard left turn as the downwind boundary of the airfield passed the port wing's trailing edge, a steady base leg on a gentle descent, another left turn on to the approach, line up with the wind-sock, throttle back, keep the nose up, get the speed off, let it sink, gently, and stay relaxed for heaven's sake, for Wallace Bacon Sheffield's sake. I held the Stearman inches from the ground, and set it down as though it were made of crystal glass.

CHAPTER
SIX

"Straighten Up an' Fly Right"

There is a sort of face which, wherever in the world it might be seen, in whatever circumstance, may be known at once for what it is — the face of an Englishman. No other race has bred that peculiarly distinctive blend of indistinctive features: the clear, pale skin, the colourless, straight hair, the equally colourless moustache, the slightly protuberant, pale-blue eyes and the expression that says something of apathy, something of complacency and very little of the man. Leading Aircraftman Culliford had that sort of face.

Alone of cadets at Souther Field, Culliford wore a pair of wings upon his chest. The story was that he had gained them in peacetime but, having forfeited his commission — for some unknown reason — must now undertake all the training again. Whether this was true or not, no one among us ever knew, but the wings — and maybe the moustache — had persuaded the Air Corps to appoint him our Captain of Cadets. This prestigious, if honorary, rank entitled him to have a bedroom to himself, and to wear a Sam Browne belt; it required that he should lead cadet parades and, assisted by a cohort of Cadet Lieutenants, exercise some minor powers of discipline; it laid on him the further duty of relaying, in language we might be expected to understand, the more esoteric edicts of the Air Corps as to how we should behave. Among these were the rules on table etiquette.

"Excuse me," said McLeod, addressing one of the two Upper Classmen at the breakfast table, "have you finished with the cruet?" Receiving a nod in return, he repeated the question to the other senior cadet.

"Sure, go ahead."

McLeod salted his eggs and conversation was resumed. "They reckon," said Lawton, "that this bloke Culliford is actually a regular Squadron Leader in disguise."

Treadaway sought permission to pour himself more coffee from the steaming pewter jug. Granted this, he asked: "What's he in disguise for?"

"Because he's a spy from the Air Ministry," said Walker, "finding oot the truth aboot The Arnold Scheme."

The waiter set a fresh rack of toast on the table. "Thank you, Aaron," said Featonby, covering a slice with butter and molasses. "I'm afraid that's utter nonsense. Spies don't go around drawing attention to themselves by wearing wings and moustaches and things."

Walker was silenced, for the moment, by this piece of logic, but Johnson, opening a bottle of milk, pursued the point. "He's got to wear his wings, hasn't he? I mean, once you've been given them, it's like, er . . ."

"Like wearing a turban if you're a Sikh," prompted Withers, "the same as old wossname at Stratford."

"Yes, the same as . . . no, you daft clot!"

"Okay, you people," said an Upper Classman. "Hold it down to a quiet roar, will you? Mr Cartwright and I are trying to hear ourselves eat."

We continued, sotto voce, without resentment of the reprimand for, considering the powers their status gave them, our seniors had treated us with reasonable humanity. As for them, their sixty hours completed, and their numbers significantly reduced by elimination (as failure to pass the course was doomfully described) they would soon be due for leave. On return from New York, Los Angeles, or wherever their fancy and their means might take them, they would be on their way to Basic Training, and 42H would become the Upper Class at Souther Field.

The table-talk now turned, as it often did, to the idiosyncrasies of the flying instructors: of the one who always stuck his chewing gum on the tail-plane, the other who never flew without his Stetson hat. "My chap," whispered Treadaway, "chews tobacco all the time, and every few minutes he sticks his head out of the cockpit and spits a great squirt over the side . . ."

"Disgusting," muttered Featonby.

"No, he's very polite about it. He always says, 'Did that hit ya, Mister Treadaway?' "

Percy Burt did not have much to say at table, nor anywhere else for that matter, and we all knew why:

neither he nor big Jim Skinner had yet soloed, and they were both near the cut-off point of twelve hours dual. Their next flight would be, not with their own, familiar instructor, but with one of the cold-eyed Army check-pilots, whose very appearance on the flying line was sufficient to invoke thoughts of Moncton tickets and goodbye to pilot's wings.

Not that going solo meant that you could sit back and relax — not for a moment. Every fifteen hours came a "check-ride" which could bring a drastic reappraisal of your chances; there were the "accuracy stages", when, closely supervised, you had to fly a pattern with geometric precision and get it absolutely right; and there was the ever-present danger of making a "ground-loop" any time you let the Stearman get crossways to the wind without sufficient speed to keep it straight with the rudder. And if, having negotiated these trials and troubles in the air, a student thought he had it made, he might find that all he had made was a mistake. He could still be "washed out", "eliminated", "get the one-way ticket", however the big goodbye might be discribed, for revealing some inadequacy, some un-officer-like quality, in his conduct on the ground. The trouble was that for the US Army Air Corps, unlike the RAF, there was no such an animal as a non-commissioned pilot: no matter how well you might fly an aeroplane if you didn't meet their standards for command there would be no wings for you in the States.

I had flown with Sheff every day since going solo, learning "Chandelles", "Lazy Eights" and "Pylon

Eights", and then going off to practice them alone. In the Chandelle ("Vertical Reversement", according to the syllabus, but no one at Souther ever called it that), you climbed until the speed dropped almost to the stall, made a steep 180 degree turn and went into a dive until the speed built up again to 120 mph, then up into another climb, another steep 180 degree turn at the top, and down again to where you started from. Lazy Eights were similar, but with the turns at the top made in opposite directions and a cross-over at the bottom to describe a figure eight. In Pylon Eights, you cut out the vertical dimension and, using adjacent electricity pylons as the turning points, flew the figure flat. The thinking was (and I believed it) that frequent repetition of these simple aerobatics helped you learn to fly with some degree of accuracy, and to feel at home with the controls.

No sooner had I begun to get these manoeuvres right, and even to enjoy them, than Sheff, as though as a counterbalance, adopted the habit of suddenly pulling back the throttle just when I was trying to concentrate on flying the aeroplance. His leisured drawl would come through the headphones: "The motor's — ah — gone kinda quiet, why don't you-all pick yo'self a field."

The knowledge that this might happen any time was calculated to make you constantly aware of what sort of landscape lay below — whether it offered a site for a forced landing. Nor was it sufficient to select the field: you had to prove that you could get the Stearman in there on the glide, and make an approach to a few feet off the ground. At that point, Sheff would either say

"Okay, give her the gun", or "Too bad, we just lost another PT-17".

Admirable as I found his lack of chatter in the air, the fact that he was just as silent on the ground was troubling me a bit. He gave no indication of what he thought about his students' flying, and I, for one, didn't like to ask. Other instructors, it was known, administered pats on the back and kicks up the backside as required: Sheff simply beamed and strolled away. Afflicted by a rare attack of self-doubt, I wrote to my mother: "I'm not sure I'm making any progress, although the aeroplane now and then does what I want it to, instead of going its own way regardless . . ."

It was, perhaps, the crisis point in the process of learning how to fly, the point at which the realisation came of just how arduous it was — not the act of flying itself, which wasn't all that difficult — but flying to order, doing it right, day in, day out, no matter how you felt. I didn't meet the crisis well at all.

For one thing, I was feeling sick about the way the Stratford group — the only friends I had in that great continent, it seemed, if not in all the world — was being reduced. Burt and Skinner never made it to the solo stage; Lawton had been washed out on his first post-solo check-ride, and the same fate stared Withers in the face. Of those who, six weeks ago, had stepped down from the coaches into Souther's sunlight, more than a third were back in Canada or on their way. The wash-out axe, like the sword of Damocles, perpetually hung over us.

The very fact that I was there, still flying, with Featonby, McLeod, Walker, Treadaway and Garrett, should have heartened me, but it didn't. Resolution faltered: I told myself that there was nothing wrong in being an observer; after all, hadn't navigation been my favourite subject, back at ITW? A quick course in Canada, and, long before the remnants of Class 42H received their pilot's wings, I would be home. Home! The very thought of England numbed me with nostalgia. If elimination were inevitable, why prolong the agony?

"May I have a word with you, Sheff?"

He nodded, and pulled a pack of Lucky Strike from the pocket of his shirt.

"I rather think I've had it here. Would you put me up for an elimination check-ride?"

He gave me a cigarette, and flicked the head of a match with his thumb-nail. "Uh-huh." He drew on the cigarette and let the smoke run down his nose. "Lotta yo' buddies — ah — gittin' washed out?"

I nodded. I could do the strong, silent stuff, too. He smoked for a while. "You-all heard from home?"

"I beg your pardon?"

"Ree-ceived any mail yet — ah — from yo' folks?"

"Oh! No, not yet. It seems to take quite a while for letters to come through."

"Uh-huh."

He went on smiling and nodding for a few minutes, then stubbed out his cigarette and, pulling on his helmet, strolled back to the flying line, where Challoner was waiting for his detail.

That afternoon, Featonby and I were sipping Coca-Cola on the flight office verandah when the Tannoy speaker boomed across the field: "Cadet Currie, report to airplane five-one on the line. Currie to five-one, that is all."

I slung a parachute across my shoulder and picked up my helmet. "Excuse me, Ron. The wild, blue yonder calls."

Featonby tilted his head back in the sunlight and closed his eyes. "Just don't make any ground-loops."

Pilot Officer Ross, conspicuous in white flying overalls, was waiting by the Stearman. The younger of the two RAF instructors on the base, he had a pleasant, freckled face and a head of curly, ginger hair a good deal longer than was permitted for cadets. He had been a student on an early British course, retained as an instructor after he had gained his wings. I noticed that his parachute was in the front cockpit. So, this was it: Sheff hadn't wasted any time.

"Currie?" he asked. "Mind if I come with you?"

I muttered an acknowledgement of the rhetorical politeness, and we climbed aboard. A mechanic swung the propeller, the engine coughed and fired, and I taxied the Stearman from the line on to the field.

"Hear me all right?" asked Ross. "Just carry on and make a normal take-off. Wizard day, isn't it?"

"Yes, Sir, wizard." If this was going to be my last flight as a pilot, I might as well enjoy it. Meticulously, I carried out the drills, and made an arrow-straight take-off. At fifty feet, I felt the stick move forward. "Right-ho," said Ross, "I have control."

The next half-hour was one long thrill — breathtaking, wonderful. Ross flew mostly at, or under, tree-top height, running beside the unpaved country roads, wheeling round the water-towers, side-slipping through the clumps of cypresses, flirting with the roof-top of a Sumter County mansion. The experience was a revelation: I knew nothing of low-flying, except that it was a deadly sin, that any student caught at it would be back in Moncton before his feet had touched the ground. And yet, it was the most exciting way to fly.

"Like to try it?" asked this ace, this superman, in the front cockpit.

Once I was sure that I could see the power-lines and phone-wires in time to hop over them, it was tremendous fun. I had never had the sensation of speed in an aeroplane before, but now, with the terrain flashing past a few feet from the cockpit, a hundred miles an hour really felt like — well, like a hundred miles an hour. A qualm, a sudden Sheffield image, suggested that there might be a problem if the engine stopped, but never mind about that, when it was such fun. Anyway, there was probably enough speed in hand to climb and find a field; if not — "Too bad, we just lost another PT-17." I settled down to enjoy whatever flying time remained to me.

Back over Souther Field at a sober 1,000 feet, Ross took control to execute a smooth slow-roll. I made the landing, taxied to the line, switched off the magnetos and the fuel, while the marshaller chocked the wheels. Ross signed the service-schedule, picked up his parachute and turned towards the office. I started to follow, but he stopped me with an upraised hand and pointed at the Stearman. "You can go off on your solo detail now," he said. "There's plenty of gas left in the tank."

I stared at him. "But I thought . . . I mean, wasn't this an elimination check?"

"Good Lord, no!" He hitched the parachute more comfortably on his shoulder. "What on earth made you think that?"

I shrugged, still staring at him. Suddenly, I felt a great surge of relief.

"Actually," said Ross, "your instructor's quite pleased with you. I try to fly with everybody, some time or another, and I just got round to you. Go on, get cracking!"

He turned away, and I heaved my parachute back into the cockpit. "I say, Currie . . ."

"Yes, Sir?"

"Keep it under your hat about the hedge-hopping."

"Yes, Sir."

"And don't go trying it by yourself, there's a good chap."

The first mail from home, forwarded from Turner Field, arrived next day. "Is Albany a town of some size?" my mother asked. "Is it near the sea? We can't find it in the atlas . . ." (There was even less chance, then, that she would find Americus, the nearest place to Souther: one cadet had already wounded civic pride by standing in Main Street and asking to be shown the way into the town.) My father, I read, was "doing his share of fire-watching at Shell-Mex House, and putting in two or three evenings and Sunday mornings with the Home Guard." The new Double Summer Time gave him longer in the garden "to grow as much food as possible and help, in a very small way, to save shipping for more important purposes." On pages torn from an exercise-book, my fourteen-year old sister Betty, reviewing the current entertainments, mentioned that she had been obliged to walk out on Solomon while he was playing Tchaikovsky with the London Philharmonic at the Albert Hall, because Pauline, her companion, "was feeling rather sick". While envying my access to a cornucopia of confectionery, she was happy to report that, thanks to a well-established liaison with the school tuck-shop, she continued to enjoy a daily bar of chocolate.

Sandy's was the letter of a girl who hadn't written many letters — certainly not love-letters — and, read between the lines, it touched the heart. I read it several times; in fact, I read them all again and, when I had, Harrow didn't seem so far away. Not half so far, I realised, as it must seem for school-mates who were serving in the desert, or in Burma, or on the Russian convoys or, worst of all, as prisoners-of-war. Ross himself, although his way of life at Souther Field had much to recommend it, would have to spend at least two years away from home. Whereas I, if I "got cracking", could gain my wings in five months' time and sail for home, rejoicing. But just what were my motives? What was I really trying to do — return to the bosom of the family and the arms of Sandy, or fly a heavy bomber over Germany? And, anyway, did either aim exclude the other? The airmen at the Old Boys' Club had periods of leave — short, admittedly, but regular — so long as they survived.

Sheff was satisfied — that's what had been said (and the thought of Ross was a reminder that his lot, at all costs, had to be avoided), and the message was "get cracking". My course was set, and life was for the living. After all, the discipline, however vexatious, was supportable, in view of the end; the food was marvellous, the weather was growing wonderfully warm; I no longer felt a total stranger in the cockpit; the ground school lessons weren't all that demanding; even the everlasting callisthenics had recently been enlivened by the wit of the instructor, a New Yorker whose opinion of the dear old Southland, and of Georgia in particular, would have horrified Lieutenant Honnicutt.

With renewed interest and diligence, I worked my way through the later stages of the syllabus — loops, rolls, Immelmann turns and accuracy stages. Looping was easy, except for the bit at the top, when there was only sky to see, and you came up against the physiological barrier of trying to look upwards and backwards to discover the horizon. The object was, in rolling, to maintain the aircraft's course while rolling through 360 degrees about the longitudinal axis; the roll was made with the ailerons, and the trick was to remember that, when on its side, the aircraft's rudders acted like the elevator and vice versa. In a slow roll, the engine stopped for a few seconds when it was upside-down, because the petrol flowed by gravity out of a tank in the top wing, but that shouldn't happen in a barrel-roll, because the path in that was shaped like a corkscrew (if you got it right), and centrifugal force fed the petrol to the cylinders. To make a turn in the eccentric way Herr Immelmann adopted, you went into a standard loop, held it at the top with the aircraft upside-down and facing back the way it came from, and made a half-roll to get your head back into the normal relationship with your feet.

In these aerobatics, it was necessary to build up some initial speed, because the required acceleration was more than the engine could provide from a straight-and-level start. Standing on the airfield, you could always tell, from the higher engine note as he dived, that someone up there was about to commit himself to putting on some "G", and everyone would watch to see what sort of spherical objects he was about to make of it.

"Accuracy stages" were ordinary landings, but made from different pieces of the sky in relation to the touch-down path: 90 degree side approach, 180 side, 180 overhead and 360 overhead. Sheff insisted on precise straight lines and square right-angles, the way we had to march around the base, although he admitted he didn't fly quite so geometrically himself. "Ah'm an ole bush-pilot," he explained, "an' Ah fly by the seat of mah pi-ants. But you-all gotta fly the Army way."

There was little room for error in these exercises, and I often needed more than what there was. Then the patient drawl would come through the headphones:

"Okay, let's — ah — straighten up an' fly right." I wrote to my mother "My instructor is in the throes of teaching me aerobatics — I'm sure it must hurt him a lot more than it hurts me . . ."

What with flying and ground school, and the domestic chores, the social life at Souther was not exactly hectic. If the class was up to schedule according to the syllabus, Open Post was granted on three evenings and one whole day a week. The amenities of Americus for an evening out were hardly worth the cost of a bus-ride into town and, on whole days off, we favoured a return to Albany, on account of the entertainments we had discovered while at Turner — the cinema, Lane's Restaurant and the bowling alley. Failing that, there were always invitations, pinned up on the noticeboard outside the mess-hall, to spend the day with a Sumter County family. If a cadet called their number, they would collect him in a limousine, lavish Southern hospitality upon him and return him to base in time for "lights out".

These invitations, however, were usually extended, naturally enough, to one cadet or a couple at a time and, so long as a nucleus of the Stratford group remained, we preferred to stick together in our leisure hours. On one solo venture to a family home, although Mom and Pop were affability personified, they appeared to take the view that I would be better pleased with the company of their daughter, a pretty girl, but feather-headed to the point of imbecility, and so coy into the bargain, that I was glad when the time came for the limousine to whisk me back to the horse-play and the banter of the barrack-room.

Featonby, it so happened, had a distant female cousin in Chicago, among whose friends was one called Ruth, who took it on herself to be my pen-pal. Photographs revealed her as a comely, young brunette with a lot of splendid teeth and a tendency to clothe herself in tightly-fitting jumpers; from her letters, she emerged as an intelligent and (despite the jumpers) modest sort of girl. Featonby's suggestion was that the promised fortnight's leave between Primary and Basic should be devoted to developing these tenuous relationships.

"As you know," he said one day at table, helping himself to a slice of pumpkin pie, "I'm not much of a one for girls — please, Butch, I wish you wouldn't make filthy noises like that — but I think it'd be a pity not to take the opportunity of seeing a bit more of America than just the State of Georgia while we're here, don't you?"

"Some of the chaps are talking about the West Coast — Los Angeles, Hollywood, San Francisco — they reckon you can have a helluva good time out there if you're in RAF uniform."

Featonby sniffed. "You must please yourself, of course, but I should've thought all that Movieland stuff was rather superficial. Chicago would be more — well, rewarding."

"Oh, sure. You're sex-mad, Featonby, aren't you?"

"Don't be ridiculous. I mean, educationally reward-ing."

"What are we supposed to use for money, anyway?" (At a dollar a day, and including two weeks' back-pay for the transatlantic voyage, I'd been paid about one hundred dollars since the beginning of the year and, of that, saved barely half.)

"We've enough for the coach fare," said Featonby, "and the girls will put us up and feed us. All we'll need is a little spending money."

"That's what worries me."

"Perhaps if you didn't spend so much on cokes and fags and juke-boxes . . ."

I licked my spoon and looked round for the waiter. "How about a little more ice-cream, Aaron?"

"You already had a little more." He tried to frown, which didn't come easily, broke down into the usual big, white grin and ladled out another helping. I was feeling rather rotten about Aaron, but the only thing to do was carry on as though nothing had happened. Despite the Air Commodore's "when in Rome" advice, and all the code-of-conduct stuff we learned at Turner, I still hadn't realised how strict the regime was. When, a week or so ago, a chance remark at table had revealed that Aaron was something of a hot-shot with the gloves, the idea of a friendly session in the gym had appeared to present a welcome change from being constantly bruised and buffeted by Garrett. Aaron hadn't seemed averse, although he merely shook his head and chuckled when I put it to him. Anyway, I approached the PTI — the cynical New Yorker — and booked the ring for two days later, at a time in the evening when Aaron would have finished with the dishes.

I'd looked forward to the meeting, and there had been some kidding about in the mess-hall: "How do I tell if you get a black eye, Aaron?" — "Same as you, but it won't show up so good." Then I was called to report to the Administration Officer.

"You're way outa line, Mister," he said, shaking his head more in sorrow than in anger. "Don't you know that? How long you-all been in the State of Georgia? Ain't no prejudice about it, y'understand — we gotta maintain certain standards, that is all."

"But, Sir . . ."

"You heard me, Mister — no box-fights with the stooward, okay. That is all. Take off."

Perhaps I should have said, "Stuff your standards", and stood firm, but I didn't. I just wasn't man enough to kiss my wings goodbye for the sake of a principle and half-an-hour's sparring. "I'm calling it off, Aaron," I said at the next meal-time. "I got cold feet — I reckon you might kill me. Sorry, and all that."

He nodded his close-curled head and chuckled softly. "That's okay, Sir," he said, leaning over my shoulder with a plate of boiled potatoes, "I figured you was — uh — asking for trouble."

From the quick gleam in his eye, I knew that he knew exactly what had happened, and we left it at that. Featonby was pleased about the cancellation, not because Aaron was a black man, but because he was a waiter. One just didn't indulge in social contact, let alone fisticuffs, with the lower classes, excellent fellows as they might be in their own way. Nor was he displeased that I had inexplicably been made a

Corporal of Cadets — an honorary rank which merely meant, so far as I could judge, that I would be held responsible, not only, as before, for my own kit and bed-space, but for that of all the others in the barrack-room as well; not only for being in the right place at the right time myself, but for ensuring that they were, too.

Another chore that came along was of a different order altogether. "There's this Patriotic Pageant, see," said the Admin. Officer, "at the High School in downtown Americus. They'd kinda like to have some Britishers along."

Visualising an afternoon's liberty, pretty girls, ice-cream and hamburgers, maybe even a barbecue, I waited expectantly.

"For to sing at them."

"Sing, Sir?"

"You goddit, Mister — sing. You can sing, caint't you?"

"Well, Sir . . ."

"Sure you can sing. What you do is, you assign some of your buddies to help y'out, and some guy to play piano — they gotta piano, see — an' you go sing."

"Sir."

"Next Toosday, half after three. Oh yeah, one other thing. You sing a number called 'The White Cliffs of Dover', okay?"

" 'The White Cliffs of . . .' " I gulped. This wasn't a current barrack-room favourite. In a singing vein, we leaned towards the top tunes of the moment: "Blues in the Night", "Chattanooga Choo-Choo", and "I Don't

Want To Walk Without You, Baby"; moving into closer harmony, a few had tackled "Moonlight Cocktail", but this "White Cliffs of Dover" thing was not within our repertoire.

"Yes, Mister?"

"Well, I'm afraid it's absolute bilge, Sir."

"Whaddya mean, bilge? Don't gimme that, Mister. It's patriotic, right? It's what they wanna hear, right? So sing it. Oh, yeah, there's another thing: the Major's gonna be there — he has a kid in High School, so sing it good. That is all."

That evening, I toured the barracks, seeking volunteers. Lawton and Challoner had sadly followed Burt and Skinner; Withers was to take the Moncton train next day. Featonby, however, with McLeod, Walker, Davison and Johnson formed a choral nucleus, and to these were added Treadaway, who could actually sing, Tiny Evans, who admitted to having been a chorister at school and, at his insistence, Garrett, on condition that he merely mimed the piece. Ernie Bower, a lank-haired, studious cadet, was recruited to "play piano".

The first rehearsal wasn't encouraging — levity continually broke out — but at least we got the format more or less agreed. After four bars in from Bower, I was to step out, front and centre, and deliver the first verse; the ensemble would then sing the refrain in unison, I would croon the second verse and, finally, a reprise of the refrain, this time in an attempt at harmony.

102

The verses were long and quite exceptionally inane, and it was force majeure alone which caused me to agree to give them voice. "If you want us to make bloody fools of ourselves," McLeod insisted, "the least you can do is be the biggest bloody fool."

It was during the next rehearsal, when we reached the memorable line about "Joy and laughter, and peace ever after" in the second chorus, that the pronunication problem made itself apparent. "Hold it," I said. "Let's get together on this laughter-after thing. You sound like a flock of sheep."

"I canna say 'larfter'," Walker growled, "I'd sound like a ponce."

"Sure," agreed McLeod, "it's got to be 'lafter'."

"No, it's an English song," argued Evans, "and Englishmen say 'larfter'."

"I don't," said Davison, "and I'm English."

"No, you're not — you're Lancashire."

I wrote the verses on the back of an envelope and studied them, at opportunity, next day — at ground school in the morning and on the flying line after lunch — although the afternoon's prospect was rather more exciting than the cliffs of Dover. There was an element of risk in what I had in mind, but the truth was that my conduct recently had been so circumspect, so unhealthily officer-like, metaphorically standing at a constant position of attention, saying "Yes, Sir", that I was beginning to find myself a very boring person. Furthermore, I had never seen a real, live crocodile.

The River Flint, on which the project centred, ran from the Appalachians down to the fall-line, passing east of Souther Field on a lazy, southward course to join the Chattahoochee River at the Floridan frontier. From there, it flowed across the coastal plain to permit its slowly-moving waters to seep into the Gulf of Mexico. I had heard it said that crocodiles abounded there, any one of which, on a sudden, saurian whim, might turn its snout upstream and venture northwards on the Chattahoochee. Such a creature, arriving at the confluence, might toss a mental coin and opt to press on up the Flint. Once there, it could surely be spotted by a low-flying aircraft out of Souther Field.

The detail was for flick-rolls, Chandelles and gliding turns, flight duration forty-five minutes, in airplane No 31, and I climbed into a sky that was not only cloudless, but looked as though no cloud had ever crossed it since the world began. It seemed to be a perfect day for hunting crocodiles.

CHAPTER
SEVEN

Crocodile Quest

A couple of rolls for duty's sake, the briefest of Chandelles, and I turned towards the Flint, singing the words of that wretched song. With the throttle fully closed, the Stearman glided down on a gently curving course, while the slipstream played a quiet glissando on the bracing wires. Gradually, the shining river widened, and the shadow of the aircraft grew enormous on the bank. I pushed the throttle open to hold the height at fifty feet and cruised on southward, with my head out of the cockpit, peering through my goggles at the water underneath.

Until that morning, all I had known of crocodiles was what was to be seen from Row "H" of the stalls at the Palladium in 1935, when a working model of the creature had devoured an alarm-clock as an entrée, with Captain Cook to follow, while Miss Nova Pillbeam, in the part of Peter, crowed with Panic glee. An encyclopaedia in the ground school library, however, had provided further data: I read that, as a rule, your typical crocodile tended to be bigger, lighter-coloured, and to have a sharper snout than your average alligator — important information, which would have had more relevance if I'd had a conception of what an alligator looked like.

> "The shepherd will tend his sheep,
> The valley will bloom again,
> And Johnny will go to sleep
> In his own little room again . . ."

Thankfully, I left Johnny to his sleep as a wedge-shaped shadow appeared on the water, near the eastern bank. Turning the aircraft sharply for a closer inspection, I glanced automatically in the direction of the turn to check the way was clear. In silhouette against the sun, a hundred feet above me, was another Stearman and, as I watched, it followed in the turn.

That putative crocodile was going to have to wait: number one priority was the status of the Stearman — dual or solo. I levelled out and looked again: there was a helmeted figure in the rear cockpit and no one in the front. All was well. I turned back to the river, and searched the water near the bank, but the shape had disappeared. Not so, the shape astern — he was still there, and edging closer. It was clear what he was up to. I could hear him now, back at Souther Field: "Right on Butch Currie's tail, old boy. Could have shot him full of holes, no trouble at all."

The dashboard clock showed that the detail had twenty minutes to run — time enough to put this cheeky student in his place and find the crocodile as well. I pushed the throttle to the stop and rolled into a steep turn to the right. The engine gave a satisfying roar, the wings flexed as they took the strain, the horizon swept obliquely past the nose. Caught off-guard, my pursuer overshot, but he reacted well: with the advantage of his height, and an even steeper turn, he recovered his position on my tail. Cheeky he might be, but clearly not incompetent. I went into a series of tight figure eights — "Ace" Currie now, jockeying for position in a fight to the death with the old adversary — the famous "Yellow Baron". Steely-eyed, silk scarf fluttering in the slipstream, I dashed a smear of oil from my goggles and flung the specially-tuned machine into a manoeuvre hitherto unknown in aerial combat. Within seconds, the Baron was at my mercy. Smiling thinly, I pressed the gun-button with a remorseless thumb. My aim, as usual, was deadly. I permitted myself a brief, triumphant laugh. "Tough luck, Baron, but we've all got to go some time." Another victory for the old Squadron, another celebration in the Mess tonight. I could almost hear the CO saying "Good show, Currie," in his quiet way, as he opened the champagne and tossed me a cigar.

The aircraft rocked as it crossed a warm air current, and the flight of fancy faded. It was 1942 again, and I was flying a Primary Trainer — rather erratically, very low, and too close for comfort to another aeroplane. Somehow, we were wing-tip to wing-tip in line-abreast formation, and I wasn't due to learn how to fly formation until the Basic stage. It didn't seem too difficult, but there was one thing that bothered me — was he formatting on me, or I on him? All in all, it seemed an appropriate moment to break off the engagement. I waved a nonchalant farewell, receiving a cool nod in reply, and turned back to the river. My playmate banked away and, when I looked for him again, he was a speck in the distance, climbing to the east.

After another ten minutes' search, I realised that this was not, after all, a good day for crocodiles. Possibly the timid creatures, unaccustomed to the noise of Continental engines, had taken fright, and turned back to the quieter waters of the Chattahoochee River or the Gulf of Mexico. Climbing to a sedate 2,000 feet, checking the landmarks, I returned to Souther Field.

No sooner had I stopped the engine on the flying line and removed my helmet, than the Tannoy called "Aviation Cadet Currie — report to Captain Pardue, on the double." Throwing off the safety-straps and leaving the parachute in the cockpit, I trotted across the tarmac to the HQ building. It would be idle to pretend I didn't feel a twinge of trepidation: this Pardue character wasn't only an Army check-pilot, he was number one, the arch-eliminator, whose lightest word filled Monckton trains. Breathing hard, perspiring freely, I knocked on his door. A voice like metal scraped on stone said: "Enter!"

The Captain had a narrow, grey face, the standard hair-style just a quarter of an inch away from total baldness, and eyes which had once belonged to a singularly ill-tempered snake; it may have been an optical illusion, but his ears appeared to be pointed at the tips. He spoke with no perceptible movement of the lips. "Sound off, Mister."

"Cadet Currie, Sir."

"What was your flight detail this afternoon, Currie?" I told him.

"You were not detailed for low-flying?"

"Er — not specifically, Sir." The snake's eyes looked into mine, hypnotically. I amended the reply. "No, Sir."

"So how come your ship was observed at zero feet over the Flint River at around fourteen-fifteen hours?"

If, at that point, I didn't actually stare at him in wild surmise, it wasn't for want of trying. I was surmising as wildly as I could. Surely no classmate could have have been so vile, so treacherous, as to squeal to the tower on his return to base — no one, for Pete's sake, could be such a frightful so-and-so! I tore my eyes away from Captain Pardue's and cast about for help, for inspiration, anything . . .

That was when I noticed he was wearing overalls, and that his helmet and goggles were lying on the desk. Understanding came like the onset of a toothache. "Was it you, Sir, who — er — observed me?"

"Right in one, Currie. Do you have any explanation to offer?"

My brain groped feebly in the gathering darkness. "Would it do any good to say that I was lost, Sir, and trying to establish my position?"

"Not really, Currie. To the best of my knowledge, there are no signposts between the banks of the Flint. Try again."

"Yes, Sir. I'd better tell you the truth."

"Why not?"

I tried to smile, ingratiatingly, but the muscles in my cheeks seemed to have atrophied. "Actually, Sir, I was looking for a crocodile."

He raised his eyebrows fractionally. "How's that again?"

"I'm very interested in natural history, Sir. Somebody said there were crocodiles in the river, and that's why I was there. Looking for one."

Captain Pardue smiled — at least, it must have been the expression that served him for a smile. "You don't say. Tell me something, Currie, did you find a crocodile?"

"Well, I thought I had, Sir. I was just going round for another look when you — er — joined me."

I was glad that he stopped smiling: it had been making my blood run cold. "Yeah. What you saw, or thought you saw, could have been an alligator or, more probably, a floating log. Crocs prefer salt water."

I attempted the appearance of a natural history student to whom some great, new truth has been revealed. "Really, Sir? That's very interesting . . ."

The metallic voice cut in. "It's kind of a pity that your last detail at Souther should be abortive."

I felt the studious expression, and the blood, drain from my face. "Last detail, Sir?"

"You know that I have no other choice than to recommend your immediate suspension from flying training."

As the words sank in, with their dread finality, I realised what a fool I had been. How infinitely preferable it now seemed to be a good, obedient cadet, however boring, than an ex-cadet! I searched the hard, grey face for some faint hint of kindness, some flicker of compassion: there was none. And yet, some effort for survival must be made. "May I say something, Sir?"

"I guess you've said enough already, Mister. More than enough." He frowned. I liked it better when he frowned — it suited him. "But okay, go ahead."

"I've only got three hours to do before I finish, Sir, and it's terribly important I should go on and get my win — well, important to me. I know the low flying was wrong, and I'm very sorry. Couldn't you possibly sort forget about it, just this once?"

He shook his head slowly. " 'Fraid not, Currie. You should know better than to ask. Low flying is an automatic wash-out offence. Who's your instructor? Mr. Sheffield? Okay, report to him. Tell him you're suspended, and why. That is all."

I saluted automatically and turned away. As I reached the door, he spoke again. "Too bad, Currie — I kind of enjoyed the tail-chase."

Sheff was sitting in the instructors' rest room, huddled in a wicker chair with his feet on the table. His hands were in his jacket pockets and, although the temperature was in the seventies, the sheepskin collar was turned up round his cheeks. He listened serenely while I poured the story out. "I'm sorry, Sheff," I ended, "I know I've let you down."

He gave a non-committal grunt, and glanced down at his watch. "What did the Captain say for you-all to do?"

"Report to you."

"Okay, you did that. Gotta nickel? Go git yo'self a coke."

The next half-hour passed slowly. It was the worst half-hour I'd ever known. No wings, no bomber cockpit. Every Stearman that buzzed across the vivid sky seemed to mock the ruin of ambition — self-destroyed ambition. "Dear Daddy, this is just to let you know that I've decided to be a navigator . . ." No, that wouldn't do. I hoped no one would see me or speak to me, wished that I could hide somewhere — crawl into a hole and pull it in behind me. Even the Coca-Cola had a vapid taste. I gazed round glumly at the ordered rows of bushes on the verges of the paths, at the neat, white buildings, shining in the sun. Sheff was standing in the doorway of the Flight Office, smoking a cigar and beckoning.

"Ain't no call to look like you-all goin' to the ee-lectric chair," he said. "We — ah — gonna make a pilot outa you yet."

As I stared into the smiling eyes, the weight of despair seemed to lift from my shoulders and I felt the blood returning to my face. "But Captain Pardue said it was an automatic wash-out."

"Yeah, well, the Captain — ah — kinda changed his mind." He tapped ash off the cigar. "There'll be some punishment to work out, but I guess you-all won't mind that, huh?"

"Gosh, no! What does he want me to do?"

He shrugged. "Guess yo' have to see the RAF Staff Officer on that."

The feeling of relief was still so strong when I stood before the Squadron Leader that I missed most of his reprimand, and it wasn't until he reached his peroration that he had my full attention. He wore a smart tropical uniform, and he seemed to have a very pleasant face. ". . . and you're damn lucky," he was saying, "not to be eliminated. I can tell you that you jolly well would have been if your instructor hadn't spoken up for you. In view of what he said, the Commandant has decided to make an exception so that you can finish the course. You're awarded fifty tours and fourteen days confinement to camp."

I'd never heard of anyone getting fifty tours before, not all at once, but what of that? "Yes, Sir, Thank you, Sir."

"Don't thank me, LAC, thank Mr. Sheffield. And take that silly grin off your face."

"Yes, Sir. Sorry, Sir."

"Now, your C.C. won't take effect until next Saturday — that's so you can do whatever it is you're supposed to do at the High School Pageant. It means you'll miss your end-of-course leave, but that can't be helped."

"No, Sir." On more critical inspection, I wasn't quite so sure about the Squadron Leader's looks. In fact, his face was slightly bloated, and the moustache was really rather a mistake.

"What do you mean, 'No, Sir'?"

"I mean it can't be helped, Sir. At least, I suppose not . . ." I was beginning to wonder about his uniform — perhaps "dandified" would be an apter word than

113

"smart". I mean, I hadn't actually had any leave since . . .

"LAC!"

"Yes, Sir?"

"Clear off, thank your lucky stars, and take my advice — stay out of Captain Pardue's way until you're on the coach for Cochran."

I followed that advice and, on 10th April 1942, arrived at Cochran Field for the Basic Training Course. The field lay in the heart of the peanut, peach and pecan country, sixty miles from Souther, between two more of Georgia's many rivers, the Ocmulgee and Oconee (so named by the Cherokee before our ancestors came south), which met, after much meandering, to flow into the ocean as the Altamaha. Macon, the nearest township to the field, stood on the fall-line to the north where a narrow belt of hills ran, in an intermittent, irregular line across the State, from Augusta on the South Carolinan border in the east to Phoenix City, Alabama, in the west.

The cadets from Souther Field — just over half the number who had begun the course — joined the survivors of other Primary Schools in the south-eastern states: Lakeland and Arcadia in Florida, Camden in South Carolina and Darr Aero Tech. in Georgia to form a Lower Class at Cochran of some three hundred students. The strength of the Upper Class, further reduced since the Primary stage by yet more elimination and a fatal accident, stood at two hundred and sixty. To the training of these courses, the South East Army Air Force (as the Air Corps had recently

114

been re-designated) dedicated Cochran's eleven hundred acres, four auxiliary landing fields, one hundred and seventy-eight aeroplanes, three thousand officers, enlisted men and civilians, twenty-two barrack-blocks, four mess halls, three operations blocks, the inevitable ground school, a complex of hangars, engineering workshops, administration offices and supply rooms, storage tanks for 135,000 gallons of fuel, a Post Exchange, a theatre, a gymnasium, three Link Trainers, a post office, a Skeet range and, for good measure, the 303rd Army Air Force Band. The lack of a swimming pool for officers, and bowling alleys for the men, had been noted and construction would be shortly put in hand. The student-instructor ratio was exactly three to one.

Tiny Evans, Featonby and I shared a barrack-room with Davison, whose good humour and stoicism had been notable at Souther, when his angelic looks and somewhat prissy manner had attracted rather more than his fair share of ragging. His were qualities of which we all had need in the early days at Cochran. Souther, in comparison, had been a leisure centre — here, we trained for fifteen hours a day at frantic pace.

In the hour before "Lights Out" on 1st May, I sat on my bed and tried to compose a letter to my mother that wouldn't read like a petition for mercy from a penal colony. I decided it was best to draw a veil over the last week at Souther, the endless marching and indescribable tedium. In the week before, when I wasn't marching, it had at least been possible to share the misery with Walker, McLeod and the burly Geordie,

Heppinstall, who were all confined to camp for misdemeanours of their own, but once their sentences were served, they had been on pleasure bent, and had left me to my solitary, footsore fate . . .

The base had been deserted, my classmates scattered across the length and breadth of the USA; even the Lower Class had Open Post. At last sweet mercy, like the gentle rain from heaven, fell on Souther Field. It came in the unlikely shape of the Officer of the Day who, having watched my laden progress from his office window for a while, strolled onto the square. "Hold it, Mister," he drawled. "At ease. How long you bin walkin' tours?"

"Five days, Sir."

"How many you done?"

"I'm on the forty-second, Sir."

He tipped his cap back and whistled. "Shoot! You sure must be one wicked kaydet."

I was too tired to argue.

"What's your name, Mister?"

I told him.

"Goddit," he said, "you're the crocodile guy. Hell, you're not wicked — you just got caught. Listen, Currie, I can't rest easy in my office while you're stomping around out here. Go walk your tours some place else, okay? Like in the sack, or any place. Just don't leave the base, is all."

Even with that happy ending, the incident in total didn't make ideal material for the cheerful, filial letter. Nor could the High School Pageant, which should have offered a more suitable subject, be described as an unqualified success . . .

Wearing our best blue uniforms, with every button shining, we had been ushered on arrival into a well-filled hall. A strong patriotic theme was established by the decorations, which included the Stars and Stripes, depictions of Uncle Sam and a beady-eyed bald eagle, numerous interesting military tableaux, and the colourful banners of the many voluntary groups with which American society is blessed. The piano was located at the far end of the hall, and Bower, when seated on the stool, had his back to the stage and was hidden from our view by a streamer, bearing an injunction to "Remember Pearl Harbor", which hung across the body of the hall.

Distantly, I heard the four bars in and, trying not to think too much about the words, embarked upon verse one.

"I'll never forget the people I met
Braving those angry skies;
I remember well as the shadows fell
The light of hope in their eyes.
And though I'm far away, I still can hear them say
'Thumbs up!' For when the dawn comes up . . ."

Bower and I finished more or less together, and the choir came in with a roar that made me jump.

"There'll be bluebirds over the white cliffs of Dover
Tomorrow, just you wait and see . . ."

It was early in the second verse that things began to
slide: I'd been so successful in not thinking of the
words that now I couldn't remember them at all. I
hoped I might pick them up on the second line, or the
third, but nothing came. I stood there, opening and
closing my mouth from time to time, while Bower,
oblivious, played on in the distance. I smiled out into
the faceless mass in front of me — at least, I tried to
smile. Still, nothing came. Somewhere out there, I
remembered, sat the Major, no doubt eyeing me coldly
and enquiring, "Who is this guy?"

"I'm terribly sorry, ladies and gentlemen", I said,
fumbling in my pockets for the envelope, "but I seem to
have forgotten the words." Inexplicably, the audience
reacted to the debacle with a round of clapping.
Wondering at this, perhaps, Bower ceased to play —
either that, or he had left the hall. I discovered that, by
kneeling down, with my head just above the level of the
stage, it was possible to see below the Pearl Harbor
streamer, although a flag-draped pillar now stood in the
way. I crawled across the stage for a few yards in total
silence — I had clearly found a way of capturing
attention — and looked again. Bower was still there,
and it was evident, from the way his head was cocked,
that he was hoping to hear from me. "I say, Ernie," I
called, "shall we try it again, from the top of the second
verse?"

Bower thumped the four bars in, and I began:

"I may not be near, but I have no fear,
History will prove it, too,
When the tale is told, t'will be as of old,
For truth will always win through.
Be I far or near, that slogan still I'll hear:
'Thumbs up!' For when the dawn comes up . . ."

Most of these golden words were wasted: on hearing the first line, the audience broke into the sort of laughter more usually evoked by someone falling through the backdrop or the singer's trousers catching fire, and this occupied them happily until the choir came in again. It was impossible to tell whether the applause that followed us off-stage was inspired by satisfaction, fervour for the Allied cause or pure relief, but subsequent comments gave a clue. "I've always said that what this Pageant needs is a comic act," boomed one stolid citizen at the refreshment table; "Sure," agreed another, "a good laff never did nobody no harm." A piece of constructive criticism came from a stout child in knickerbockers and a spotted bow-tie: "You were swell, buddy," he piped, proffering a plate of crackers, "but, say, when you blew your lines, why didn't you just 'la-la' them? That's what I do . . ."

Deciding that a brief outline of the Pageant, pared of the pantomime, could go into the letter, I went on to recall what else had happened in the last few days at Souther. There had been the final flying detail when, by tradition, to complete whatever minutes remained of the scheduled sixty hours, instructor and student exchanged roles. Having never flown in the front

119

cockpit before, I was too absorbed in the sensation and the new perspective to treat my mentor, as did some, to a taste of his own medicine. When we had flown our fifteen minutes, in mutual accord, Sheff made the landing from a whistling side-slip, crabbing in with crossed controls and straightening out for the touch-down. It was certainly an effective way of losing height in a hurry but, for a moment, it did cross my mind that the great man (who seldom flew the Stearman from the rear) had found himself a little too high on the approach.

Featonby and Davison were waiting on the flying line with our farewell gift. For all we knew, Sheff had a dozen travelling clocks, but he put up a convincing show of gratification, and added his valedictory advice. "Ah'm an ole bush-pilot. Damn, that's all Ah can do!" He beamed at each of us — a beacon, steady among ships in transit. "Where yo' goin', you-all gotta do better'n that — fly the panel, fly formation, fly the range — lotsa things. But don't you-all forget the seat of yo' pi-ants, yo' hear me?" He broke off into chuckles, and we all shook hands . . .

I put the gist of this into the letter and signed off as a bugler of the 303rd Army Air Force Band sounded "Taps".

CHAPTER
EIGHT

Fly the Army Way

"Let's not keep our head in the cockpit, Cue-ree," suggested the instructor. "Let's try and cultivate the roving eye."

I tore my eyes away from the instruments and looked around the sky — even that seemed strange, seen for the first time through the perspex of a canopy. Everything was strange: the panel, the cockpit, the engine, the airfield and its landmarks. And not least strange was the instructor.

First Lieutenant James M. Sena, of the 323rd Basic Flying Training Squadron (one of five such units based at Cochran Field), was a thin, hunch-shouldered man with a sallow complexion, a large hooked nose and more teeth than his mouth was meant to hold — which may have been the reason why his characteristic expression was a snarl and why he tended to salivate every time he spoke. His reading of my name, despite occasional correction, was invariably "Cue-ree"; what with that, and the absurdly inept "Butch" used by my classmates, I had begun to wonder whether I existed in my own right any more, or had become a phantom thing, a creation of other people's minds — a thing that ate, flew, ran from place to place, crying "Yes, Sir," on command, that only lived in someone else's life.

The Vultee Valiant was real enough — a solid, low-winged monoplane with a wide fixed under-carriage, a tall tail-fin and a Pratt & Whitney engine with twice the 220 horse-power of the Stearman's Continental. No more the thrill of open cockpits — the Vultee's sliding canopy eliminated draughts; no more speaking-tubes or Very signal flares — this aeroplane had intercom and radio; it also had wing-flaps with which to change the airflow and reduce the landing speed. The Air Force had designated it the BT-13a and, although the instructors called it, among themselves, "The Vultee Vibrator", to me it was a marvellous machine.

It's impossible to tell why, of similar objects, similar experiences, one should be more pleasing than any of the others. If you go into a sports shop and try some of the cricket bats, one will be just right; listen to a record programme on the radio, one tune in a hundred will stay with you for life; walk into a dance-hall and look around the floor, one girl will be the pick. When my mother asked in a letter, "Do you actually enjoy flying?" I thought how strange it was that, after seventy hours or so spent in a cockpit, I'd never asked that question of myself. Until I flew the BT-13a, I wouldn't have been certain, but now I knew that I enjoyed it very much. There was no telling why, no more than you could tell why you picked that bat, remembered that tune or wanted that girl, but many times, flying that aeroplane, I felt the same sort of elation which, on a

122

summer morning three years earlier, had made me burst out singing . . .

It was when the days were long and peaceful, and pavements shimmered in the heat; when gardens beckoned brightly and trees were dense with leaf. Since leaving school, I'd never stayed long enough in an occupation to make any sort of mark: a few weeks' clerking in High Holborn, and a few more at a Sudbury Hill bank, had been enough to convince me, and my employers, that office work was not my cup of tea. Lured by the outdoor life, and a weekly wage of one-pound-ten, I drove in succession a delivery-van for Biggs the Butchers, an ironmonger's Morris that smelled of paraffin and soap and, peaked-capped and sober-suited, a company limousine — but not for long. (You may sneer, proud chauffeurs, stiff with swank and steeped in scandal, flicking dusters over gleaming bonnets as you wait your masters' will, but I tell you this — the driver of a van has much more fun.)

It was not unknown in Pinner, Eastcote and Hatch End for people to keep a bottle or two about the house, and my next employer, Mr Oliphant the wine-merchant, strove to meet their needs. The doorstep contact was agreeable: whether I carried a crate of Tolly ales and a hundred Woodbines to a semi, or a dozen Gilbey's Gin and a Craven "A" carton to a mansion, there was always a welcome to be had. It was no concern of mine if they paid by cash or on account, or, to be truthful, if they paid at all — it was always fun to serve them.

Fun it was not to Mr Oliphant who, back at the store, took the whole operation very seriously indeed. But life was good, especially in the mornings, and I had to sing about it as I went about my work, so it may have been a lapse in concentration, or the small financial interest that I had in empty bottles, that made me turn my head to check the damage when a double bend in Eastcote brought a sound of breaking glass. When I turned back, a lamp-post stood directly in the way. There was a clang of metal as the standard toppled, and a shattering of glass. I switched off the ignition, lit a cigarette and brooded. I had reluctantly decided that the lamp-post could not be held to blame when the smell of gas drifted through the shattered windscreen. I put out the cigarette and tried to wriggle out between the seat, which had slid forward, and the wheel, which was pressing on my chest.

"Excuse me," said a lady, appearing from a gateway, "I wonder if you'd like a cup of tea?"

"That's very kind," I said, "and could you possibly phone the gas company and tell them that their lamp-post has collided with a van?"

The gas-men came and rid the atmosphere of gas; Mr Oliphant followed them and rid himself of me . . .

The sky over Cochran, although free of static hazards, tended to be crowded with Vultee Valiants, and Lieutenant Sena's counsel was entirely sound. It certainly made sense, before indulging in manoeuvres, to ensure that no one else was in the piece of sky that you proposed to use — plus a little more for mother's sake.

The Lieutenant sent me solo after five hours' dual — a little less than average — and it was then that we started to get down to business. That was the time of change, the metamorphosis, from simply learning how to fly to really learning how to operate a Service aeroplane. Cochran Field, as Sheff had adumbrated, was where you learned to fly the Army way — the panel, formation and the range. Formation details were the only ones in which the Lieutenant didn't insist upon the "roving eye", because then you had eyes for no one but the leader, and his eyes did the roving for the rest.

At the start, we flew in "Vics" of three with an instructor in the lead; well spaced across the runway for the take-off and landings, tighter at the operating height. All you had to do was to keep station on the leader's wing, first in level flight and then in gentle turns. The right place to be was a wing-span and a half away from the leader, with your aircraft's nose abreast of and below his tail. To be there wasn't difficult — it only required manual dexterity, perfect judgement and a proper blend of fearlessness and care — to stay there demanded rather more, and my first attempts didn't attract Lieutenant Sena's praise. The trick was to anticipate how much power was needed on the outside of a turn — on the leader's left when turning right and vice versa — and how much less on the inside of a turn. A formation turn, before we got the hang of this, tended to become a straggling echelon, with the outside aircraft way behind the leader, and the inside man way out in front. It needed constant, small adjustments of

125

the throttle to keep the speed just right, and a nice, light touch on the controls to maintain something worthy of being known as a formation. It was all too easy to tense up and start to over-correct, jerking the throttle open and shut, and using the rudder like the pedals of a bicycle, which only led to streams of perspiration and a very bad formation. "Let's loosen up," advised the Lieutenant. "The ship will fly formation if you don't keep trying to stop it."

Flying the panel was another ball-game altogether, or — in Lieutenant Sena's oft-repeated words — a needle, ball and air-speed game; if he had added compass and altimeter he would have totally defined the gamut of an instrument flying exercise (IF to the RAF). Access to the sophisticated gyro-driven instruments — the artificial horizon and the direction-indicator — would have made it all too easy, so they were masked for the duration of the flight. I flew the panel for eight hours dual, and another eight on "team rides" with a fellow-student, taking it in turns to fly and keep a lookout. It wasn't my favourite exercise: to climb into a shining, sapphire sky, with the State of Georgia like a living map below, and then to pull a hood across the cockpit and live with dials and darkness until the man in front was satisfied seemed a very masochistic sort of thing to do. "Sounds horrid, darling," wrote my mother: she was right. But there was reason to be grateful, in the years to come, that Lieutenant Sena made me do those horrid things.

Compared with the discipline of patterns and the panel, the regime on the ground was not too harsh. It was true that some cadets, and I was one, picked up demerits like squirrels hoarding nuts, but this was either due to ignorance of rules, which was never an acceptable excuse in any Service, or naughtiness — testing out the system to see what might be got away with. Garrett's exploitation of this area, in all apparent innocence, was a case in point. When the last call came for lights out and no talking in the barracks, it meant exactly that: the Captain of Cadets and his Lieutenants snooped around to make sure that it did. Garrett, in the middle of a rambling, rumbling reminiscence of his days in Bristol, was silenced by a figure, stooping by his bed, who asked in a whisper: "What's your name, Cadet?"

"David," Garrett answered, huskily seductive. "What's yours, dear?"

Major Knight, Director of Cadets, was responsible for discipline at Cochran Field. A tall, imposing figure, his face invariably shadowed by a large pith helmet (a souvenir, perhaps, of service overseas), the Major paced the base alone, seeking someone to harass. In this, his favourite ploy was to hypothesise an irrational situation to which he required a rational response. "Take a brace, you men," he rasped, materialising on the path in front of us. We stiffened to attention and, at his further bidding, "sounded off".

The Major addressed himself to Evans. "Okay, Mister. You're in the sack in the barracks, and you observe that a blue-assed baboon is occupying the next bed-space. What action do you take?"

Evans giggled uncomfortably, until the stony stare got through to him. "Currie sleeps next to me, Sir. I probably wouldn't notice any difference."

That earned him two demerits — one for levity and another for an insult to baboons. The question passed to Featonby, who declared that he would immediately report the incident to the Officer of the Day: one demerit for buck-passing. Walker, like Evans, would notice nothing, but for the reason that he was always so exhausted by the rigours of the training that a whole zoo in the barracks wouldn't awaken him: two demerits for evading the issue.

"I'd tell the creature it was in the wrong berth, Sir," said McLeod, "and direct it to the Officers' Quarters."

Oddly enough, the Major merely snorted, turned on his heel and strolled away. He continued to be known by all as "The Bullshine King" but the Stratford group decided that he had a sense of humour — of a sort.

The meal-time discipline was stricter than at Souther — you didn't speak unless spoken to, kept your eyes straight ahead and elbows in — but no one complained about the chow, which was almost monotonous in its munificence. One meal in the mess-hall, according to the record, consisted of 3,700 pork chops, 48 gallons of peas, 3,000 potatoes, 212 pies, 4,000 clover-leaf rolls, 30 pounds of butter and 270 gallons of lemonade. That was lunch for 1,200 men — in the UK it would have fed 4,000 people and, on the Atlantic, seamen were dying to maintain that meagre ration. There weren't many squawks about the table discipline.

At last, an Open Post was granted, and I set out to hitch-hike to Souther for the day. Sheff had insisted on parting: "You-all be sure to come back an' see us, yo' hear," and I had promised. Furthermore, John and Paul Braund were in training there with 42J, and I longed to see a face from home.

It was the usual vivid, airless morning. In the standard rig of Army shirt and slacks, and the white-flashed cap, black tie and shoes which proclaimed the RAF cadet, I struck out in a southerly direction as though going for a stroll, but trying to convey by something in my bearing that I wasn't so mad about strolling as to refuse a lift if it were offered. It wasn't an easy posture to maintain, and I was grateful when a limousine pulled up in a cloud of dust, and the near-side door was opened by a red-haired man in a bright check shirt.

Cruising southward, my benefactor revealed that his name was Julius J. Parker, but that the world knew him, as must I, as plain "J.J.". I wasn't to think of thanking him for the ride, because, being concerned in selling agricultural machinery, travelling the length and breadth of the deep South, he spent many lonely hours at the wheel of an automobile, and was truly glad of somebody to talk to. He was further gratified to note that I was British because, in his opinion, the British were a most remarkable race. To exemplify this view, he cited William Shakespeare, Florence Nightingale and Winston S. Churchill, whose own mother — as he guessed I knew — was a daughter of the Union. It so happened that his favourite movie actress was Miss

Greer Garson, from Britain, whose playing of "Mrs Miniver" he rated as swell. It might surprise me to know that Bob Hope, the comic actor, was in fact a Britisher. Why, his own maternal great-grandfather had first seen the light of day in Nottingham, England.

Steering expertly with two fingers of one hand, he took a wallet from his hip-pocket and selected a number of photographs depicting Mrs Parker and several infant Parkers engaged in a variety of leisure activities, all of which appeared to afford them great enjoyment. With each photograph, he provided a comprehensive run-down on age, weight at birth, distinguishing marks, hobbies, academic record, eating habits, future prospects and such characteristic sayings as he judged to be of a particularly amusing or socially significant nature.

Turning to a broader theme, and inviting me to help myself to an assortment of confectionery in the glove-compartment, he passed the economic record of the Roosevelt administration in revue. He was able to excuse many of its shortcomings on account of the delusions of grandeur to which politicians were prone, and their general remoteness from the grass roots of American life; try as he might, however, he couldn't take so lenient a view of the State legislature, the activities of which he could only ascribe to criminal lunacy and a wholesale commitment to graft. To support the war effort was one thing — why, he himself had invested in War Bonds to the limit — paying taxes to feather the nests of those bums in Atlanta was quite another, and enough to turn a guy to drink. And, speaking of drink, if I were to reach into his travel-bag in the back seat, the chances were it would be found to contain a quart of Bourbon and a couple of tumblers.

Lulled by the whisky and the warm stream of chatter, I fell into a comfortable trance as the countryside drifted by. "J.J." insisted on driving to the very gates of Souther Field and, when I protested that he was going far out of his way, he would have none of it: if I could come this far from home to fly for democracy, he was not the guy to leave me standing on the highway. Having extended an open invitation to visit the Parkers in Columbus any time, he gave me in parting two packs of Chesterfields and the advice not to take "any wooden nickels", which I took to be more in the nature of a catchphrase than a cautionary allegory, because his style hadn't come through as that of one who always looked before he leaped. Rather, he had that instant brand of friendliness which, as I was learning, was typically American — so different from his distant English cousins, who would share a train compartment with a fellow man for hours with no more social contact than the first suspicious glance.

Just such inhibitions cramped communication with Wallace Bacon Sheffield when we met. "I'll always be grateful to you, Sheff," was what I should have said, "you made sure I didn't throw it all away when the going got a little less than easy, and you saved me from the crocodile disgrace; you showed me how to fly by the seat of my pants, and now I can do it your way and the Army way, and I love it, and thank you very much."

What I did say was: "Featonby and Davison send their regards and all that, Sheff. Is Mrs Sheffield quite well?"

I tracked the Braunds to the sports field and waited for their game of volley-ball to end. John came at the gallop, whooping, to thump me on the back; Paul, following sedately, gripped me by the hand. That was just as I remembered them: John the happy extrovert, clumsy as a puppy and bubbling with fun: Paul, steady-eyed and thoughtful, picking up the pieces John had left behind. The differences between them now were, if anything, more marked, but to be with them again brought back our days together — making the most, with John, of being young and carefree, while still aware, with Paul, that growing up must happen.

When I'd heard their news of home, we talked about the training. I tried not to enthuse too much about the BT-13a and we looked towards the future. "Will you try for fighters?" Paul asked. "That's what we intend to do."

"Not me. You can't win wars with fighters — it's bombers you need for that."

"Fighters are more fun, man," said John, "don't you think?"

"If it's fun you're after, you should have joined ENSA. Come to think of it, you'd be jolly good at that. I mean, you always make me laugh."

He threw himself upon me, and we wrestled for a while. Nothing had changed — we were evenly matched, equally unskilled, neither one in earnest and, as usual, Paul told us to desist. As we talked, walking to the barracks, I realised that they both expected to be officers, if they passed the course and got their wings. Of course, they had the makings — grammar school, matric, qualities of leadership and plenty of self-confidence — and I had two of those myself — but I didn't share their confidence, nor did I want to, for the fear of Ross's fate was with me still. A consoling thought was that the USAAF didn't make instructors out of Sergeant Pilots, and my tally of demerits — a record for the course at ninety-two — should stand me in good stead. And yet, a doubt remained: Lieutenant Sena had referred — sarcastically, perhaps — to the case of George A. Custer, the demerit king of West Point in his time, who had not only been commissioned but had followed a spectacular career, until the nasty episode with Crazy Horse and company beside the Little Bighorn had brought it to an end.

I'd gone so far as to confide the problem in my father, who had replied that it was something I must work out for myself; he had added, however, that he would do his best to help financially if I were to be commissioned. That he expected an officer to be needier than a Sergeant had surprised me — I had thought that it would be the other way about.

I sat on John's bed while they showered and changed into flying kit. "When you're commissioned," I said, "do you have to buy your own uniform?"

John towelled his flaxen hair. "I don't know, man. I wouldn't be surprised."

"They give you an allowance," said Paul, "but that won't cover it — not if you want to get anything decent."

"What do you mean, decent?"

"You know, from a decent tailor — not just something off the peg."

My one civilian suit had come, quite unbespoke, from the shop near Roxborough Bridge, where Fred, the outfitter, cigarette dangling from his lower lip, would find something to fit you from the rack and invite you, as a friend, to watch a naughty, home-made movie in the flat upstairs. No doubt Burtons would suit me just as well, and probably without the need to watch a movie. I concluded that my father's thought had been inspired by something more than tailoring expenses, and remembered how my cousin Charlie Dixon, MC, in reminiscent mood, would ruefully joke about his RFC mess bills. Exile, penury, the burden of authority — why would anyone want to be an officer?

It was too much to expect another "J.J." to come along on the journey home, but I never had too far to hike before someone stopped to help me on the way and, by early evening, I had found the drug-store in Macon where the group had planned to gather. As I approached the table, Walker sprang to his feet, barking "Tay-hut," and the others stood erect. "That's okay, men," I drawled, to humour them, "don't bother to get up, just kneel."

"Take my seat, Kaydet Lieutenant, Sir," McLeod requested.

"Let me light your cigarette, Sir," begged Davison.

"Would it be all right if I licked your boots, Sir?" asked Garrett.

"Will you no kick my backside first, Kaydet Lootenant?" whined Walker.

I accepted that suggestion, and a mêlée ensued which brought the proprietor to the counter, crying "Take it easy, fellers, whaddaya say?" I bought a hamburger and a chocolate-milk, and Garrett put a nickel in the Wurlitzer.

"I don't want to walk without you, baby,
Walk without my arms about you, baby;
I thought the day you left me behind,
I'd take a walk and get you right off my mind,
But now I find that
I don't want to walk without you, baby . . ."

As the song came through the speakers, soft and plaintive, I probed for the truth. Stranger indeed than fiction, it emerged: I was to rise above the friendly ranks of fellow-students to stand beside the haughty Captain of Cadets and, in that hierarchical limbo, to have the duty of enforcing the very rules I found so difficult to keep. The more I thought of it, the more I felt constrained to sing along with Dinah Shore, because Cadet Lieutenants walked alone, clad in Sam Browne belts and spurious authority, unloved by other men.

"I don't know why you're so darned miserable about it," Featonby snorted. "I reckon you've been jolly lucky."

"How on earth do you make that out?"

135

"Well, you're practically a cert for a commission, so long as you don't make a complete mess of it."

"I don't want a commission. I want to go home."

"Look at it this way, Butch," said McLeod, "you won't have to walk any more tours. That's something, isn't it?"

"Why not?"

"Cadet officers don't walk tours, you clot. They just stay in their rooms for an hour."

We debouched into the bright, wide streets of Macon in search of entertainment. On the roller-skating rink, we practised line-abreast and line-astern formations, echelons to port and starboard, and changing into arrowhead. The bowling alley was a new diversion, strange to everyone but Garrett, who claimed that, on West Country fairgrounds, he had knocked a million ninepins down between his boxing bouts. Featonby set his cap straight on the middle of his head, the better to maintain a perfect balance. "I think you'll find," he said, "that ten-pin bowling calls for a little more skill than your old skittles."

"Shove off," Garrett growled. "Give us a pill."

The echoing white alleys called to mind the winter cricket school in Chiswick, where the coach, Jack Durston, would set a wooden block behind your feet if you retreated from the bowling, and Harry Lee would roll up gentle off-breaks, crying "Come forward, young 'un, head over the ball — smell 'er!" But there had been no gangs of coloured boys at Chiswick, emerging like inky demons from the pit, to set the fallen stumps up as they set the pins up here, or to roll the balls back

136

up the alley to the bowlers — that would have made the coaches raise their hoary eyebrows!

The group decision was to round the day off with a visit to the dance-hall, and I was glad of that. So far, apart from the odd perfunctory embrace, I had been faithful to the memory of Sandy (it seemed a thousand years since we had parted — oh, the taste of salt tears on her lips!), and had no real intent to break that faith, but some relief from constant male society was overdue. As we approached the pay-box, the pounding of the rhythm section sounded promising, exciting. We exchanged anticipatory grins. "Two bits, soldier," said the girl.

Baffled, Garrett inspected the coins in his hand. "How much, miss?"

"Give her a quarter, stupid," Heppinstall advised.

"Why didn't she say so?"

Inside, the band was playing "Blues in the Night" to a half-full house. Two girls were dancing together — one wildly pretty, the other a tall, haughty-looking wench. Just Featonby's type, I thought, and nudged him in the ribs. The crooner took the microphone and held it to his lips as we moved in.

"My Momma done tol' me
When Ah wuz in knee-pants,
Ma Momma done tol' me 'Son,
Ah been in some big towns, an' heard me some
    big talk,
But there is one thing Ah know:
A woman's a two-face,

137

A worrisome thing who'll leave you to sing
The blues in the night . . .' "

During the intermission, Featonby provided Coca-
Cola. I asked the pretty girl her name.

"Huh?"

"Your name — you know, what people call you."

"Cindy Lou."

"No, really?"

"Sure, why not?"

"It's a very pretty name, but . . ."

"But what?"

"Well, I didn't know it was a real name — I thought
it was a sort of fictional name."

She was watching me narrowly. "Hey," she
exclaimed, "you-all are from the No'th!" She turned to
her companion, who was establishing a cool rapport
with Featonby. "Hey, Belle, honey, these boys are
Yankees!"

Despite the fact that Cindy Lou's acquaintance with
geography petered out at the 49th parallel, we got along
quite well, and by ten o'clock that evening we were at
our ease in the girls' back-street apartment — Featonby
and Belle in one room, Cindy Lou and I in the other,
with Jimmy Launcefoot's band playing something
restful on the radio. Now and then I opened another
can of Schlitz or toyed with the odd peanut while
Cindy Lou, under the influence of red wine that
smelled like rusty tin, grew demonstratively friendly.

In a limited experience of situations such as this,
where physical advances seemed to be in order, I had

usually taken it on myself to make the running, but my pace was far too slow for Cindy Lou. Can number three was barely empty when she snatched it from my hand and threw it over her shoulder; switching off the overhead light, she then proceeded to remove, not only all her own clothing, but most of mine as well. The next few minutes were full of heavy breathing, mounting spasms of muscular and glandular activity, and not a little noise. And when things had just begun to settle down, further disturbances broke out. The door swung open with a crash to reveal Belle, stripped for action, hair about her shoulders, with what appeared to be a riding-crop in her hand. "Switcheroo," she carolled. "Okay, Cindy Lou, let's all move around one place!"

I caught a glimpse in the doorway of Featonby's face, stiff with disapproval, before Cindy Lou slipped away and Belle was on me like a harpy. "Make me know it," she breathed, "c'mon, honey, thrill me, bite me, kill me . . ." Closely entwined, we rolled off the divan on to the floor, while Belle emitted squeals and groans in equal, piercing measure. Of the sensations running through me, lust was lying third, lethargy was disputing it with panic for the lead, and panic won.

Disentanglement called for superhuman effort, but panic often helps in that respect. I found my clothes and banged on Featonby's door. "Ron! We've just got time to catch the bus," I croaked. "Must go, girls, thanks awfully for the drinks and everything . . ."

As we trotted through the half-lit streets towards the bus-stop, Featonby, who was seldom known to use a naughty word, allowed himself a couple. "Just my bloody type, you said," he panted. "My bloody type be blowed!"

We caught the last bus to Cochran in the nick of time, and flopped into our seats among a noisy chorus of suggestive comment. "She darned near strangled me," said Featonby, still in a complaining vein, "and she wanted me to whack her with a stick."

"So?"

"Well, what do you take me for?"

"Not like you to disappoint a lady, Ron."

"And what about you? You darn well panicked — just as I was getting on nicely with what's her name."

"Me? Panic? Don't be daft." Thinking about it, I was sure I hadn't panicked — not really. In a fix like that, you recognised the danger, and either took off smartly or stayed and faced the music — the fly-or-fight reaction — and which course you selected depended on how you felt about the danger and on what sort of chap you were. That wasn't panic — that was looking at the options and exercising judgement. I explained all this to Featonby as the bus bounced back to the base, but his attention fell a good deal short of rapt.

Next day, on the cross-country flight — now, that was more like panic. But only because there were no options open — none, at least, that I could see — and all the signposts were pointing to disaster.

Six hours of the syllabus were allotted to daylight pilot-navigation: three flights, each a little longer than the last and with another turning point or two. This, my first cross-country, was to Siloam and return — a trip of about 240 miles. The Lieutenant, supervising

140

preparation, had watched closely while I drew a track-line on the map, measured out the distance and the bearing, applied the wind speed and direction to find a "course true", converted that into a "course magnetic" by allowing for the difference between map north and polar north, and added a factor for magnetic deviation to find a "course compass" — the one that I would try to steer.

The estimated flight-time to Siloam had worked out at fifty-five minutes, with three degrees of drift to starboard, and ten minutes less coming back, with drift to port. Allowing for five minutes in the pattern at each end gave a total airborne time of an hour and fifty minutes. There were a few small townships on track to use as check-points, and Lieutenant Sena had suggested that if the worst came to the worst — as he had little doubt it would — I could always read the place-names on oil-tanks or water-towers. "Okay, Cue-ree, on your way," he had said, "and don't kid yourself I'll worry if you don't come back. I got other stoodents."

The outbound flight went well. Every check-point came up right on time and bang on track. The little airfield came in sight ahead of schedule, so the head-wind must have slackened off a little on the last part of the route, and I toyed with the idea of making a couple of circuits to let the clock come round to ETA, but discarded it as being too exquisite a refinement, and thumped the wheels down on the strip exactly fifty minutes after take-off.

It was the first landing I'd ever made away from base, and the excitement of the moment struck me as I taxied round the field. It was as though I had assumed a potent, new identity. No one at Siloam knew me for a struggling student, with less than thirty hours on type, flying his first cross-country. So far as Siloam knew, this visitor, who had made so masterly an approach and landing, and now taxied with such effortless command, was some great ace whose whim it was, when not engaged on more momentous missions, occasionally to drop in on a humble, rural landing-strip, flying incognito in a basic trainer. Passing the sheds and huts which were the only signs of habitation on the field, I opened the canopy and would have waved a gracious hand, had there been anyone to wave at. Siloam had not turned out in strength.

At the crosswind halt, I made the take-off checks aloud, in an imitation of Lieutenant Sena's sing-song style. The BT-13a rose like a bird, and gathered flying speed. I turned on course for Cochran, thinned the fuel mixture and settled in the cockpit for a comfortable return. This cross-country stuff was really pretty simple, after all.

An hour and fifty minutes later, I was 5,000 feet above a large expanse of nowhere and checking the fuel-gauge with increasing frequency. It was quite inexplicable: the return flight should have been perfectly straightforward (or, as the outbound journey in reverse, straightbackward). The only possible explanation was that, in my absence, Cochran Field and its environs had been moved. Admittedly, I hadn't adhered exactly to the flight-plan: you could hardly pass a huge column of smoke, towering in the distance, without a brief investigation of its cause. That had taken me thirty degrees off track for a quarter of an hour or so — a little longer than intended — and all I had found was a pile of burning motor-tyres, but I'd made the detour good by a sixty-degree correction to get back on track. At least, I thought I'd made it good.

That was where my troubles had begun. Checkpoints had failed to reveal themselves, and the more I searched for them the less familiar the landscape had become. Ten minutes after ETA at Cochran, I had turned back and tried it on reciprocal. After all, if an enormous airfield, complete with runways, hangars, towers and barracks, could vanish while your back was turned, there was a chance that if you turned again it might have reappeared. It hadn't.

My next move was to fly a series of wide figure-eights on either side of the track. No sign of Cochran; quite gone from the State. Or perhaps it was I who had quite gone from Georgia — perhaps some unforeseen change of wind had wafted the aeroplane over Alabama, or Florida, or even South Carolina. That would explain why nothing on the ground equated with the map — or vice versa. This precious document, carefully folded to show the route, was strapped across my thigh. Extracting it, I tried to unfold it with one hand. The map resisted. I went at it two-handed, at which the aeroplane commenced a climbing turn to port. Correcting this, I dropped the map, which — in accordance with Sod's Law — slid underneath the seat.

143

A fully-grown gorilla might have reached it; I, even with the longer, kitbag-dragging arm, could not — not without undoing the harness-straps. While I was doing that and recovering the map, the aeroplane amused itself. Resuming level flight, I caught sight of a water-tower, not far away to starboard. Acknowledging Lieutenant Sena's prescience, and with a feeling of relief, I put the nose down in a shallow, diving turn.

The air was warmer at the lower altitude, and I pulled back the canopy; the map was promptly snatched out of my hand and disappeared. To know now from the bold, white letters on the water-tower that it supplied a tiny burg called Hawkinsville could not have mattered less. It was then that I began to call for help, quietly at first, apologetically: "Cochran Field, this is Three-Zero-Six. Are you receiving me, over?" A whisper of static was the only answer. I tried again more urgently: still no reply. I resorted to a general appeal: "Any station receiving this transmission, please acknowledge, over!" Nothing. "Any aircraft receiving this . . ." Normally, the sky was thick with aeroplanes, and the R.T. full of chatter. I hardly dared look at the fuel-gauge any more: the needle had been knocking on the bottom of the scale for some time.

If this contingency was ever covered in the navigation class, I must have missed it. It was true that, up to now, I'd come to think of myself as something of a hot-shot in the subject, and hadn't always paid such close attention as the instructor might have wished, but I was sure I would have noticed if he had said, "On arriving at a condition of total lostness, this is what you do . . ."

Perhaps that's what he was going to teach the afternoon, ten days ago, when we persuaded him instead to let us listen to a broadcast on the radio from London, and to hear that robust voice of England with the growling, rounded vowels, echoing among the desks and blackboards of the sun-baked classroom. "What is there," he had asked, "in front of Hitler now? We are on his tracks, and so is the great Republic of the United States. Already the RAF has set about it; the British, and presently the American, bombing offensive against Germany will be one of the principal features of this year's world war. Now is the time to use our increasing superior air strength to strike hard and continually at the home front in Germany, from which so much evil has leaked out upon the world, and which is the foundation of the whole enormous German invasion of Russia. Now, while the German armies will be bleeding and burning up their strength against the two-thousand-mile Russian line, and when the news of casualties by hundreds of thousands is streaming back to the German Reich, now is the time to bring home to the German people the wickedness of their rulers, by destroying under their very eyes the factories and sea-ports on which their war effort depends . . . Therefore tonight I give you a message of good cheer. You deserve it and the facts endorse it. But be it good cheer or be it bad cheer will make no difference to us; we shall drive on to the end, and do our duty, win or die. God helping us, we can do no other."

But where did duty lie in this predicament? Not in flying round in circles until the aeroplane and I made a

145

hole in the landscape — that would be no use to Mr Churchill, and none to me. Nor in baling out, to let the BT-13a go make a hole all by itself — the USAAF might take a stuffy view of that. The more I thought about it, the more certain I became that if there were ever a case for a forced landing, this was it — and a forced landing in earnest, with my skin as forfeit if I foozled it.

The voice of Wallace Bacon Sheffield seemed to drawl, "Okay pick yo'self a field," and I turned the aeroplane around. It was thanks to Sheff that I had noted the right spot a few miles back. Only slightly terrified at what had to be done, I re-examined it: a good five hundred yards long, reasonably flat, with no power lines or trees to hamper the approach, no livestock to baulk the landing. If it wasn't the finest landing field in all the Southern States, it was good enough. I enriched the fuel mixture and flew a standard 360 degree overhead stage, which brought the aircraft in about ten feet above the scrub-wood, downwind of the field. As it settled on the tawny grass, a shadow swept across the ground ahead. I looked up: there was the US Cavalry, at the gallop, guidons flying and bugles blowing, in the nick of time to rescue the outpost and to save its occupant from scalping by the savage Sena. The Cavalry came in the shape of a BT-13a — one with the appearance of being flown home to Cochran Field in time for chow. I pushed the throttle open, turned the landing run into a take-off like a golfer's follow-through and chased that BT-13a.

146

Two hours and thirty minutes after taking off from Siloam, BT-13a No. 306 pulled up on the flying line at Cochran with its engine faltering. The Lieutenant required an explanation. "Whaddaya mean 'slightly lost?'" he snarled. "You are exactly one hour, forty-five minutes late. We took 'Airplane Overdoo' procedure here — do you have any idea what that involves, Cue-ree?"

"You promised not to worry if I was late back, Sir."

He scowled horribly, and I moved quickly to another tack. "What I can't understand is why nobody answered when I called on RT."

"Presoomably on account of you were too goddam low. Radio waves don't bend, it's line of sight propagation, okay? Ya gotta have altitood." He frowned for a moment. "I oughta chew your ass off, but I guess you learned your lesson." I threw up a salute and turned to go. "Oh yeah, Cue-ree, one more thing . . ."

"Yes, Sir?"

"Ya get three more demerits."

"For getting lost, Sir?"

"For losing your goddam map."

CHAPTER
NINE

Sena the Vigilant

Whether it was the BT-13a, his instructor, or a bit of both McLeod couldn't get along with, we never discovered. Whatever the reason, Mac was eliminated. If we all missed his handsome looks and easy-going style, and I especially the bond we had formed against what the charge-sheets described as Good Order and Air Force Discipline, Walker was disconsolate, for he had lost a boon companion as well as a compatriot.

Ungratefully, those of us surviving chafed together at the long grind of training. It seemed that we'd been in America for ever, and yet we were only half-way through the course. News of the thousand-bomber raid on Cologne, and of another on the following night — almost as severe — against Essen, did nothing to cool the heat of our impatience. And hot we truly were, for now high summer roasted Georgia like a chicken on the grill. These were days for frying eggs on pavements, days when you learned to touch no door-knobs in case they burned your hand, and when you took a shower in the middle of the night to get cool enough to sleep.

Late in the evening of 10th June, we waited in the barracks for a night-flying detail. In the next room, a radio was tuned to London, and Foden's Motor Works' band, with a brave blare of trumpets and a thump of drums, was playing "The British Grenadiers". Featonby, in underpants and vest, looked like a cadaver awaiting the autopsy. My reflection in the mirror above the writing desk showed perspiration running down my face like the rivers of Georgia on their courses to the sea. When I joined the chorus, it was in a dry and feeble voice.

"But of all the world's great heroes
There's none that can compare
With a tow-ra-ra-row, ta-ra-row-ra-ra-row
With the British Gre-he-he-nadiers!"

"I wish you'd shut up," said Featonby, "and tell those blighters to turn that row down."

"That row is coming from home, Ron. You're not very patriotic, are you?"

"Of course I am. I just want to get a nap before we go flying."

The night detail was flown from a Fort Valley landing strip known as Harris Field, and it was supervised by Captain Wendell M. Van Sickle, Officer Commanding the 323rd. Tall and well-built, with the swarthy good looks of a "B" movie gang boss, the Captain perched nonchalantly on the back of a chair, controlling operations through a hand-held microphone wired into an aircraft radio. His instructions were augmented by another officer, standing beside him with an Aldis signal lamp. The strip was floodlit, but once off the ground it was as though you had emerged into the black-out from a well-lighted house. It was best to forget about a real horizon and to concentrate instead on the artificial one on the panel — this was the time when the investment in IF began to pay a dividend. Your eyes would gradually become accustomed to the dark, at least to the point where you could just tell earth from sky. Then you would start to make out the difference between degrees of darkness, between the woodland and the fields, the rivers and the roads. When the moon was up and anywhere near full, there really was no difficulty about night vision. It was a monochrome world, but with contrasts well-defined, and all that you lacked was some colour in your life.

Flying at night, with that transition past, was absolutely fine: unprovoked by solar heat, the air soon lost its turbulence, and lay serenely on the bosom of the earth. It was a stark environment, but with few distractions, and that made it easier to concentrate on what you had to do. It also seemed to me that the night was benevolent, sympathetic to my efforts, forgiving of my faults, and hiding my shortcomings in a veil of secrecy.

However illusory those impressions were, they were comforting to me, and they really helped. Captain Van Sickle smiled upon me, and even the Lieutenant could scarce forbear to cheer. "That wasn't too lousy a pattern," he enthused. But, when I failed to suppress the smallest smirk of satisfaction, he became himself again. "Let's not get hysterical," he said. "I wanna see

150

how you make out on wing-lights — I'll have the Captain kill the floods."

The solo night cross-country — a two-hour flight to Alma and back — was scheduled for 25th June. On previous brief departures from the pattern it had seemed that night navigation was easier than day: the flashing letters of the civil airways beacons beat water-towers and oil-tanks every time. All you had to do, according to the cognoscenti, for a carefree ride to Alma was to stick with the Jacksonville Light Line. However, since it had been shown that the cadets of our class had ways of getting lost that no one else had thought of, the Cochran Field instructors mounted a massive anti-lostness campaign. They deployed an aeroplane to patrol, like cowhands riding herd, on both sides of the route. It was one of these outriders who identified and reported that strange phenomenon in the skies of Georgia — a cloud. The cross-country was cancelled straightaway.

Grumbling about this was rife among the ranks, but the Director of Flying had good reason for his action. Little clouds grew bigger in southern summer skies, and first night cross-countries were best flown in the clear. He would have also had in mind that the accident graph had shown nineteen in May — four times the Cochran average. If it didn't show a sharp decline in June, he might not be wearing the stars on his shoulders very long.

To maintain the momentum, the Lieutenant sent his students back to night take-offs and landings, with flood-lights and without, with wing-lights and in black-out. So far, he hadn't seemed dissatisfied with the way I was flying — the patterns, the accuracy stages, the formation and the panel; the night flying, as yet, had not caused him to snarl. He'd never liked my aerobatics, and I had no quarrel with his judgement: I knew I had no flair for those aerial contortions. "Cue-ree," he had commented, "you fly a slow roll like a barrel roll, you fly a barrel roll like a Chandelle that got lost on top, an' you fly a snap roll . . . Hell, you don't fly a snap roll. I figure you just shut your eyes an' hope."

He was also disappointed with my performance on the skeet-range. I was all right on the target range, with a rifle or a Tommy gun, but with a double-barrelled shot-gun, shooting at clay pigeons, I was a total flop. If I averaged one hit in five pulls, that was a pretty good day. Really this was none of the Lieutenant's business, but he wasn't one of the general run of flying instructors who, by and large, were content to see their students on the flying line and to leave all other training to the specialists. Not so Lieutenant Sena: he was liable to appear on the parade ground, on the soft-ball field, at Link Trainer practice — anywhere — to "see how you make out", and he wouldn't spare himself if he believed you stood in need of exhortation or advice. It was therefore no surprise to find him lurking at my elbow when another salvo of Bakelite ash-trays went hurtling past the firing-point unscathed. "Aw, c'mon, Cue-ree," he muttered, "you can do better'n that. Swing the foresight on through the flight of the goddam skeet, and squeeze that trigger."

"Yes, I know that, Sir, but I don't seem able to bring myself to hurt them."

"Listen, Mister, this isn't for laffs. This is an ee-ssential phase of your goddam training in the US Army Air Force, okay? You sure as hell won't get to be a pursoot pilot if you can't shoot skeets. So let's get the lead out of our ass."

The sibilant content of that little speech had exceeded his saliva threshold, and he wiped his chin with a khaki handkerchief. I reloaded thoughtfully: here was an opportunity I could not afford to miss. From Cochran Field, the class of 42H would be irrevocably divided into two streams — streams which, in due course, would lead to one of the RAF Commands. One stream would go from here to an Advanced Course on single-engined Harvards, and would eventually become the fighter pilots of the future; the potential bomber pilots would go with the other stream to fly twin-engined aircraft. The point was that the flying instructor's recommendation would be crucial when the Air Force made its choice. Praising the name of Sena the ubiquitous, the vigilant, I took careful aim, and never hit another ash-tray — not even accidentally.

It was in Macon that I found a really worthwhile target. She stalked proudly past the window of a down-town bar-room, where I was sipping a solitary Schlitz, and she put the scene around her completely out of focus. She wore a dress of soft, blue taffeta which followed the curves of her figure like a tracing. Her hair was as black as a rook's wing, smooth and gleaming, and her flesh was the colour of a good, strong cup of

153

tea. In one white-gloved hand she carried a wide, straw hat and, from the other, a large, black handbag swung beside a shapely leg. She swept past the window looking neither right nor left, and I gazed after her, entranced by the gentle, reciprocating swing of her lissom buttocks. When she had disappeared from view, the scene reverted to normality. In the glaring, dusty street a tired mongrel dog was trying to decide whether or not to leave its mark upon a lamp-post. Behind me, the bartender was studying the funnies in a paper, while the Wurlitzer played "Chattanooga Choo-choo" for the fifty-thousandth time. Two customers in overalls sat morosely at a table, thick elbows planted in a field of empty beer-cans. I turned back to the window and the world grew bright again: she was coming back.

I swallowed the beer, took a deep breath and pushed the swing-doors open. I'd been practising a slow, shy smile like Gary Cooper's and, saluting the approaching vision, I tried it on now. She looked at me as she might have looked at a piece of graffiti on the wall, and walked on by. The mongrel dog, pausing in its deliberations, regarded me with greater interest than she. I hurried in pursuit. "Excuse me, Miss," I said. "I wonder if you could direct me to the cinema?"

She stalked on in silence, but her eyelashes had flickered. "It's a lovely afternoon, isn't it?" I suggested. "Too nice for going to the pictures, really. You don't mind if I walk along with you, do you?"

She didn't answer, but suddenly broke into a gurgle of laughter. Her teeth were as white as cloud-tops in moonlight. We paced on up the street together — I, chattering but saying nothing; she, silent but saying a lot with her beauty — until the pavement and the buildings fell behind us. There, just out of town, she paused and faced me. At first, I couldn't understand her sing-song drawl, and begged her pardon.

The forehead, on which she stretched a tiny frown, was broad, the grey-blue eyes enormous; she had a little button nose, nostrils a millimetre wider than the norm and on her upper lip there was the softest trace of down. "Ah said you-all better not foller me no further."

"Why not?"

"'Cos Ah ain't fixin' to git in no trouble counta you-all, white boy."

Gazing at her, I realised that I'd passed this way before, with Aaron the waiter, back at Souther Field. This lovely creature was probably a quadroon or a mulatto and so, for all her beauty, she lived on the wrong side of the colour bar. "I'm English," I said. "I'm not concerned with your funny rules. I just like pretty girls. What's wrong with that?"

There was another flicker of a smile before she could get the frown on board again. "Honey, it ain't no funny rule, it's just the way it is. In this town, black and white don't mix none, none at all."

"I bet your parents don't believe that," I said boldly, "or maybe your grandparents."

She tossed her head, and the gleaming hair danced and settled back again, like a curtain moving in the wind. "Sure," she said, "and there weren't noth'n' but trouble came from that."

"What's your name?"

155

"Ain't none of yo' business what's my name."

"Mine's Jack."

She rocked with the gurgle of laughter once again. "That ain't no name! Thass what you-all hitch a truck up with. That ain't no man's name."

"Well, it's mine, and I'm a man." She gave me a long, slow scan, up and down and up again. I hoped I wasn't blushing, but it rather felt as though I might be. "I'm a pilot, in training."

"That so?" She transferred the straw hat to her handbag hand and examined her fingernails, clearly underwhelmed by my revelation. Then she looked up. "They call me Lalange," she said.

"That's a lovely name. Is it French?"

"Guess so."

"Why's that?"

"Y'all sho' do ask a lotta questions, pilot boy. Ah'm Creole gal, thass why."

As I gazed into her eyes, the haunting tune came back to mind: Duke Ellington's band, with Cootie Williams on trumpet, playing "Creole Love Call". That old record was 4,000 miles away, on my bedroom shelf at home. For a moment I wished that I were there as well, not in this torrid land, making a fool of myself with this exotic girl. But I was on Open Post, and content to let foolishness be my guide. "Are you going home? I'll walk with you."

"Ah already tol' you-all . . ."

"And I told you. I'm English, and you're awfully pretty."

Home was in a straggling row of tumble-down shanties, with roofs of rusty corrugated iron, three miles out of town. That she should live there was as much of a paradox as that lovely flowers should bloom on compost-heaps. Chickens, pecking in the dust, scattered as we passed, and the whites of eyes gleamed through unglazed windows. Beyond their range, in the shade of a magnolia tree, she kissed me, but when the soft yield of her lips aroused my ardour she gently broke away. "You-all ain't gonna start no pettin', now. Go find yo'self a nice, white girl — there's plenty around, down town."

"Not like you, Lalange."

She stroked her palm across my face, and smiled the moonlight smile. "On your way, pilot boy. An' you-all take care of yo'self, ya hear?"

I turned away, and picked a path through the chickens, knowing that I left her queen of all that she surveyed — proud, serene and beautiful in all the squalor of her realm. I was in retreat, but with no sense of being defeated, and I felt relaxed and happy as I walked back to the town, humming "The Creole Love Call" as I went.

The bus dropped me at Cochran as the current Captain of Cadets was alighting from an enormous limousine. I studied the stately blonde girl at the wheel: for all her costly clothes, her motor-car's six cylinders and the haughty Afghan posing in the rear, Lalange was more desirable than she would ever be.

The Cadet Captain, one Michael Rennie, had been known before enlistment as a movie actor. This

157

circumstance, with its connotation of wealth and of glamour, set him even further apart from the herd than did his rank. It had also caused him a little embarrassment, when a film called *Ships with Wings*, in which he played a leading role as a dashing naval pilot, was shown at the Post Theatre. The rumour was that the darkly-handsome Michael wasn't quite the best and brightest student-pilot on the base, and his daring exploits on the screen gave rise to happy laughter, and his eventual demise in a heroic operation was greeted with applause and requests for an encore.

Amusing as that occasion had been, it was surpassed for entertainment value by the Farewell Squadron Dinner for which, on 1st July, the instructors of the 323rd took over "The Green Lizard" to speed the graduating students on their merry way. Despite the spate of accidents in May, the results of the course had not been all that bad: forty-five eliminations, one fatal accident and fourteen students held over, for one reason or another, to join the ranks of 42I (the first mixed course of British and American cadets).

As 42H's graduation was a week behind schedule, the end-of-course leave had been summarily cancelled; nevertheless, we were a happy group at table. After five substantial courses, which included roast beef, green peas and a brave attempt at Yorkshire Pudding, toasts were sonorously proposed to the President of the United States, His Majesty King George VI, the United States Army Air Force and the RAF. After Captain Van Sickle had delivered a suitably sententious speech, and Lieutenant Sena a witty one, in his sardonic, salivating style, informality set in. Drinking, much of it sustained and concentrated, became rife, and was combined with outbreaks of horse-play, during which, at a late stage of the party, the starboard wing of Cadet Lieutenant Culliford's moustache was ceremonially removed.

Lieutenant Sena, protective to the last, collected his own students in a quite corner and busied himself about us like a hen-bird with her fledglings, providing a carefully-calculated supply of alcohol, cigarettes and sweetmeats, until the night was done. Then he loaded us into his Packard and drove us home to bed.

"They gotta lotta rookie instructors at Moody," he told me as we parted, "guys who aren't long graduated themselves. Hell, they don't have much more air time than you do, Cue-ree. So remember everything you learned here and at Primary. Read the book so you can say it in your sleep, then fly by it. I don't wanna have some smart-ass sonofabitch Advanced instructor callin' me and askin' how come I recommended this dumb Britisher for multi-engined ships, okay?"

CHAPTER
TEN

Mother Moody's Rest Camp

"If hell should ever cool," I wrote to my mother, "the Devil could always move his HQ here." Although the average temperature was in the mid-eighties, that hardly constitued an inferno: it was the humidity which so oppressed the atmosphere, and made Moody Field a very sticky spot. This was partly due to the many cypress ponds which pitted the otherwise featureless plain, and partly to the fact that, to the east, the plain became the eerie Okefenokee swamplands, whose miasmic waters overflowed into the Swanee River of the song.

"How nice a cool, drizzly Autumn day will seem when you come home," replied my mother. "Of course, we are all longing to see you, but my feelings are somewhat mixed — to tell the truth I feel each move brings you nearer the war — but I realise we shouldn't get much further if everyone felt like that . . ." In her heart, she hoped that I would be commissioned and stay, as an instructor, in the States, but she understood why I took a different view. Certainly, the first few days at "Mother Moody's Rest Camp" made me long to shake the dust of Georgia off my shoes. It wasn't so much that I'd lost a few more friends when the single-engined stream had gone to other schools: the further fragmentation of the Stratford group didn't seem so painful as it had at Souther Field. I knew now that the Service wasn't like the family, a school or a cricket club, and that relationships with flying men were best kept nice and loose — that was a salutary lesson to have learned, and one I was to remember in the future. No, it wasn't the absence of Treadaway and Walker that was hard to bear, it was the presence of the Moody Upper Class.

Our seniors hitherto, at Souther and at Cochran, had all been RAF cadets: here, they were USAAF, and they made it their business to make sure we knew the difference. They subjected the students of 42H, with every evidence of zeal, to the process of organised bullying, euphemised as "hazing" and hallowed by authority. Within the terms of the code, these budding officers and gentlemen could impose their will on their juniors with total impunity, making up the rules as they went along, and punishing infringements by whatever means afforded them amusement at the time. Some unfortunate cadets were given scalding shower-baths, some merrily flogged with sopping, knotted towels; one, so careless as to pass Old Glory at a quarter-mile's distance without a salute, was hoisted to the mast-head like a human pennant; little Charlie Davison, for once sufficiently provoked to show resentment, was tossed with his belongings from a first-floor window of the barrack block; Heppinstall and Garrett were seldom out of trouble, and even I, behaving with superhuman circumspection, finally fell foul of the regime, and was required to circle the parade ground at the double, dressed in every garment in my kitbag, layer on layer, until one of the young demi-gods cried halt. Featonby alone appeared untouched by hazing, and went about his business, nose in air, as though the Upper Class did not exist.

If the veterans — the re-mustered soldiers and the ex-policemen — had still been with us, with their own ideas about what discipline should be, there might have been a riot in the ranks, but most of them had fallen by the wayside, at Primary or Basic, and those who had come this far didn't feel inclined to stop now. If hazing were the price of travelling on, we had to pay, but didn't make us like the fare-collectors.

However dispassionately you viewed them, you would find it hard to see a Sena or a Honnicutt among the Upper Class (although you might possibly distinguish a Pardue or a Knight). Physically there was little wrong with them: on the whole, they were taller, broader, better nourished than we were. But they strutted when they walked, grated when they talked, had a total lack of grace and suffered from a shortage of that much-redeeming gift — a sense of humour.

Apart from the predations of the Upper Class, the humidity, the flies (which, though smaller than at Cochran, were more numerous and virulent), and the fifteen-hour day, Moody was a splendid place to be; after all, there weren't many ills, at twenty years of age, which didn't respond to three good meals a day and restful sleep at night.

The pine-fringed camp had been constructed, late in 1941, on the Lakeland flats, a thousand-acre site to the north-east of Valdosta. It was the Mayor of that town, one Daniel Ashley, who had been the moving spirit in persuading the Air Corps to build an air-base there. Now, Moody Field, with its wide paved streets, lined by water oaks and flaming pink crepe myrtle, its theatre, church and hospital, its telephone exchange and sewerage plant, and its branch line of the Georgia and Florida Railway, was better-equipped and a lot better-looking than many Southern towns.

Two hundred aeroplanes, of three different types, were based on Moody Field: the Curtiss AT-9 Jeep, with two 280 HP Lycoming engines, the Cessna AT-17 Crane, with a pair of Jacobs 225s, and the North American AT-6 Harvard, powered by a single 550 HP Pratt & Witney Wasp. All had folding landing-gear, and each had some additional, interesting refinement — automatic pilot, cabin heat and ventilation, fuel tank cross-feed, beam-approach facility and constant speed propellers. Four thousand people lived and worked at Moody to keep them flying. There was hangarage for all, and four good runways — two of concrete and two of asphalt — linked to a spacious parking apron by many a mile of wide paved taxiway. As for such leisure time as there was, two bus companies vied to provide an hourly service into town, conveniently halting in Ashley Street, where stood, by happy chance, the Daniel Ashley Hotel.

Gradually, as 42H were drawn into the machinery of Moody's training system, there was less contact between us and the Upper Class: while we were on the flying line, they were in the ground school, and we changed around at midday. Hazing largely petered out. To complete the eight-week advanced training syllabus, a student would spend seventy hours flying as pilot, and twenty or so on "sandbag time" — as watch-dog for a colleague who was flying the panel; he would spend a hundred and twenty-five hours in the classrooms, twenty hours at drill and — horror upon horror — forty hours at callisthenics. What with this, the flight briefings, the Link Trainer practice, parades, barrack chores and orderly duties, time didn't hang heavily on hand.

Featonby, at his desk in the barrack-room, began to read from a document: "Tactics and techniques of air attack — seven hours," he chanted. "Theory of bombs . . ."

"Shut up, Ron," I requested. "Can't you see I'm busy?"

"Lying flat on your back in the pit?"

"I'm thinking."

"You — thinking? Don't make me laugh. What about?"

"Rita Hayworth, of course. What else is there?"

He sniffed. "You'd do better to take a bit of interest in this."

"I doubt it. What is it, anyway?"

"The ground school syllabus. 'Theory of bombs — eight hours, identification of naval vessels . . .'"

"That'll be useful, over Essen."

"'. . . nine hours'. We're not all going on bombers, Butch. Some types might go to Coastal. 'Armament — sixteen hours, Employment of aviation in the Army — five hours . . .'."

"There's a chance for a bit of Rita Hayworth time."

"'. . . Maintenance engineering — ten hours . . .'"

Featonby droned on: signal communications, firearm refreshers, "code practice and blinker" — he translated that as Morse buzzer and lamp — use and care of parachutes . . .

By then, I was asleep. Next day, however, the Ground School Director elaborated further. "The conditions in which you men will operate in Europe," he declaimed, "call for the greatest possible skill in navigation. As bombardment pilots, it will be your responsibility to check the accuracy of your navigator's calculations at all times. Therefore, your navigation studies will be extended to twenty-eight hours."

He glanced at his clip-board and a shadow of anxiety passed across the sunny landscape of his face. "Tests have shown that your knowledge of aircraft identification is kind of sketchy, so extra time will be devoted to this area. The good noos is that you will not be assigned to studies applicable to US kaydets only, and time will also be redooced on some type studies, such as chemical defence and ant-eye aircraft operations, that have been adequately covered in your pree-liminary training in the UK."

The ground school had a nucleus of qualified tutors who put their subjects over well, but there weren't enough of them to go around, and many sessions fell to flying instructors, inexperienced in classroom work, borrowed from the Squadrons to help out. With them, I sometimes had the feeling that my footsteps were being guided through the fog of ignorance by men who, if not so blind as I was, were blessed with only partial sight at best. The sensation of being inexpertly instructed was a new one and, when it also happened in the air, a touch alarming. The Lieutenant's words of parting often echoed in the cockpit when, from the corner of my eye, I saw the stiffly anxious face of an instructor learning how to fly the aircraft under the pretence of teaching me.

To stop an engine in the air at Moody, either in the AT-9 or AT-17, was an exercise that few instructors ventured. It could have been that they mistrusted the aircraft's single-engined performance or their capacity to handle it, or both, but the fact was that flying on asymmetric power — a necessary skill, as I and many others were later to discover — was something Moody didn't regularly teach. Nor did every flying instructor practice what the classroom teachers preached about techniques for getting more miles to the gallon from the aircraft engines. Furthermore, they favoured "wheeler" landings with the twin-engined aircraft, which was not the way that Sheff or the Lieutenant had taught me to land — "three-pointers", every time. Wheelers were easier, there was no doubt of that, and it was true that with a vast expanse of runway at the pilot's disposal there wasn't any need to skimp on landing runs at Moody, but to touch down on three wheels, right at the point of stall and just across the threshold, was the essence of a landing, and far more satisfying. Certainly, with an eye to the future, it was the better practice to maintain.

It was common knowledge that the AT-17 — Moody's most-used type — was not the best twin-engined trainer in the world. This was not the students' judgement — we had no comparative criteria — but we heard the flying line gossip, and this was that the low-powered Cessna didn't fly high enough or fast enough, that its undercarriage was too flimsy to stand up to constant practice landings, that its Jacobs engines lacked cooling gills and its propellers the pitch controls which bomber aircraft had, and that its brakes overheated at the slightest touch. Another snag, according to the scuttlebutt, was that you might find some difficulty in abandoning the aircraft, especially if you happened to be wearing a parachute, and there was circumstantial evidence for this: from two mid-air collisions, high above the Moody pattern within the past few months, none of the eight participants had returned to have his parachute re-packed.

Prompted by these incidents, the USAAF had banned formation flying in the Cessna, and employed the other twin — the Curtiss AT-9 — to fill the gap. The AT-9, however, although it offered some prospect of exit in emergency, wasn't altogether free of little snags; in fact, among the staff, it wasn't far behind the AT-17 in the most unpopular aircraft stakes. It had proved to need more maintenance than two of any other type, and its performance on take-off was so sluggish that it couldn't be used on the auxiliary fields. Its behaviour in a glide was better than a kitchen-stove — but not a lot. A further criticism was that the cockpit door-posts couldn't have been more ingeniously located if the designer had set out to provide the maximum interference with the pilot's field of vision, and that this tended to make pattern and formation flying — the only exercises for which the AT-9 was now employed — rather more exciting than they need be. However, it was nice to know that, if you did get in a tangle, there was a chance you wouldn't still be sitting in the aircraft when it hit the ground.

These minor matters provided ample small-talk for flying line waiting-time, but they didn't really bother me at all: I'd reached the stage in learning how to fly when everything about the air and the aeroplanes was marvellous. Boyhood dreams were daily being translated into real life and already, in my mind, where ignorance constantly strove with arrogance for mastery, I was half-way to the status of an ace. Every aircraft was a wonderful new toy, and to find fault with one of them was as unthinkable as, ten years ago, it would have been to criticise the latest acquisition to the Hornby train set that my father had set beneath the Christmas tree.

I preferred to have these playthings to myself, flying alone and uninhibited, unwatched by other eyes, but at Moody only the Harvard was flown solo. In the twins, two students always flew together, taking turns to be pilot and co-pilot. It was during such an exercise, on mutual transition, that the latest rumour about the AT-9s was put to the test. My co-pilot was Aviation

Cadet Dennis, whom Featonby suspected of being lame in the brain. We had been in the air for about three hours, and it was his turn to make the approach and landing. He sang out the drill in the transatlantic accent which it pleased him to adopt in cockpit conversation, while I followed him through on the check-list. "Gas — right-hand tank; undercarriage — down; check indicator — down; mixture — rich; pitch — fully fine."

He came down the approach at an airspeed of just under 100 mph — a little faster than he needed, but there was no harm in having 10 mph in hand for mother's sake. He put the flaps down, keeping nice and steady on the runway's centre line, and used a touch of motor to maintain his speed. The approach had all the makings of a decent landing, and I sat back, relaxed, watching the runway grow wider and foreshortened as the AT-9 lost height. The main wheels touched, the tyre rubber squealed at the friction, and the aeroplane ran on, losing speed as Dennis pulled the stick back to get the tail-wheel on the ground. So far, so good: if all the instructors made wheelers, who was I to criticise? Dennis was entitled to his momentary smirk. It was only when the AT-9's full weight bore down upon the wheels that his landing started to go wrong.

Then came a nasty sinking feeling as the landing gear collapsed, a succession of expensive noises as the metal of the engine nacelles and the fabric of the fuselage were scraped along the concrete, and a splintering of wood as the propellers buckled up. The quick deceleration tried to throw me through the windscreen,

169

but the harness wouldn't let it. As I turned off the fuel-feed and the ignition, the controller's voice, devoid of all expression, drawled through the headphones: "One-zero-five, this is Moody Tower. When you have finished your slide, clear to the right, over."

Dennis's eyes, always slightly protuberant, were now almost popping from his head. I judged him to be principally concerned about two matters: whether he would be held to blame for what had happened and, if so, exactly how an unjust world might punish him. If the cost of replacing the AT-9, he would be calculating, were to be deducted from his pay, it would take about a hundred and fifty years to clear the debt, with nothing to spare for chewing-gum or popcorn. I was glad to note that he retained sufficient grip on himself to kick the rudder to the right. The squealing hulk of airplane 105 slewed off the paved part of the runway and came to rest on the asphalt shoulder. In the ensuing massive silence, I unclasped the harness-straps and offered a sympathetic word. "You've really done it now, Dennis, haven't you? Jolly bad luck. Never mind, you'll probably make LAC u/t navigator — that's if they don't chuck you out of aircrew altogether."

"What the hell do you mean?" he asked, boggling horribly and forsaking the cockpit accent. "The wheels just folded up — you saw that yourself!"

"They usually do when they're not properly locked down."

"Christ, why didn't you tell me? You were supposed to check the drill . . ." His eyes swivelled wildly to the panel, and a sickly grin appeared on the perspiring face. "You bastard, they bloody well were locked down!"

I pushed the starboard door open. "I should hop out, if I were you. This thing's liable to burst into flames at any moment. Then all you'll make is LAC u/t harpist."

By now, they were well-used to belly-landings at Moody Field, and the clamorous arrival of the fire-truck and the ambulance was quickly followed by that of a crane — to drag the hulk away. There wasn't any fire, the only injury was to feelings, the only penalty to tramp across the airfield carrying our parachutes, and the entire episode was reduced to insignificance by what was to happen later in the day.

From the southernmost turning point on the transition flight, near the coast of Florida, we had seen the storm clouds' anvil-tops towering white in the distance, high above a rumpled pillow-heap of cumulus. Far below, a dark skirt of nimbo-stratus trailed across the gulf. We had been taught enough about cumulo-nimbus to view the scene with some respect, and to be glad that it didn't lie on our route to Moody Field. "Cu-nim is trouble," we'd been told, "with a capital 'T'. Severe icing, violent turbulence, intense electrical discharge, hail. Do not, repeat not, tangle with cu-nim."

Whether the seven RAF cadets and the USAAF instructor who were killed that night knew what they were tangling with, thirty miles south-west of Moody Field, would never be discovered. They must have been aware that thunder was about — the weather briefing would have surely forecast that — but briefing was one thing, flying was another. They might have been already flying in cloud, following the compass through those rumpled pillows, and entered the storm-clouds unaware that they were there; they might have seen the shape of clouds ahead and not known what sort they were until too late; or, since the aim of the exercise was to reach the destination, they might simply have decided to press on anyway. After all, they may have figured, if they let little lumps of cloud turn them back over Georgia, they might not make much headway in the skies above the Ruhr.

Next day, the dead cadets were named: Stevens of High Wycombe, Lamont of Glasgow, Holmes of Kimbolton, Howcroft from Yorkshire, Longbottom of Liverpool, Platt of Leytonstone and Pinsent of East Barnet. It was a front-page story in the *Valdosta Times*: "A violent tropical storm arose, and the planes were placed in a very precarious position . . . eye-witnesses who saw them fall to earth said they seemed like huge balls of fire dropping from the heavens . . ."

Moody Field became extremely weather-conscious for a while. One week later, my co-pilot and I were peremptorily recalled from somewhere over Alabama and, looking at the lurid sky ahead, weren't too unhappy to cut the mission short. On that occasion someone back at base had taken the decision to recall all aircraft and cancel flying for the day. Sure enough, there was another storm that evening, brief but violent, with torrential rain and hurricane-force winds which blew trees and hoardings down, ripped the roofs off houses and tore away the power-lines.

The plain had been scorching in its hottest spell of weather for nearly forty years. "The temperature," reported the *Lowndes County News*, "has averaged a steady 100 in the shade all week, so warm in fact that half of the citizens were ready to quit South Georgia and sojourn in the mountains until the intense heat-wave came to an end."

One day's Open Post gave insufficient time for a quick trip to the mountains, let alone a sojourn, so with Davison, Holmes and Jackson (Derbyshire men, who shared the next barrack-room and a fondness for brass bands), Featonby and I took a taxi to Twin Lakes, south of Valdosta, for a quiet, cooling day beside the water. A raft was moored some fifty yards from shore, which Featonby and the others reached in a flash. They clambered on board, laughing as they shook the water from their eyes, pushing each other back into the lake, and calling me to join them.

I was not a good swimmer; to be more forthcoming with the truth, I was a poor swimmer, and my laboured breast-stroke moved me through the water almost imperceptibly. Nevertheless, I reached the raft at last and clung to the side, regaining breath and strength, while the others practised the crawl, the back-stroke and the butterfly-stroke, as smooth as any fish. When the spots before my eyes had cleared, I dragged myself aboard and lay back on the warm wood in the sun.

Featonby's face appeared alongside, the wet hair plastered to his skull. "You shouldn't try so hard," he told me, "to keep your face out of the water. You only need to lift your head every other stroke or so, to take a breath."

"Push off," I said, by way of thanks for the advice. "I'm resting."

Time passed; the raft swayed gently as the swimmers came and went. When I woke, the lake was as empty as King Arthur's, before the ghostly barge appeared to ferry him away into the myths of time. The sound of Jackson's radio, drifting across the water, suggested that the swimmers had returned to shore. They might even now be eating the hamburgers and drinking the cold beer; the time had come to leave this floating oven-plate.

I had neither the skill nor the inclination to emulate their swallow dives and, furthermore, I had always started swimming from a standing start. However, unless the lake were to be drained or the raft towed to the land, there only seemed to be one way to reach the shore. I took a deep breath and slid overboard. To say I sank like a stone would not be accurate, for stones make no attempt to stay afloat; I made every attempt, I put out every effort, but the result was basically the same. As I fought the unavailing battle that every drowning man must fight, the waters of the lake invaded every body orifice. Twice, they played a little game, allowing flailing limbs to propel me to the surface for a convulsive gulp of air, and to feel the brief heat of the sunshine on my face. The first time that they dragged me down again, I still was not convinced that I was going to die and, struggling, was angry at my incompetence and failing strength; next time, I knew the point was made — I was a rotten swimmer, and I would drown.

A hand was strong beneath my head, and a voice was talking through the roaring in my ears. The voice was that of Featonby, and the rather acid tones were those he used when he was cross. "All right, I've got you. Don't grab me like that, just lie back, will you?"

When I had grovelled at the lake-side for a while, regurgitating water, he offered a towel. "I was only kidding, you know," I croaked, "only having you on."

"Oh, yeah?" He was picking up a number of colloquial expressions. I didn't think they suited him at all.

"I wanted to see how you'd react." I began to towel my head. "Actually, you reacted quite well."

Featonby, simpering slightly, turned away. It was hard to tell who was the more embarrassed, the saver or the saved. I remembered that his sweetheart, in a phone-call to my mother, had talked of her relief to know that we had stayed together; she had felt that I, more worldly-wise than he, would see that he didn't come to harm.

That afternoon, at the USO Club in town, we received a friendly welcome from the Director, Major Langer. This amiable officer made it his affair to enquire as to the welfare of visiting cadets and, where he felt that it was needed, offer help. His further practice was to take a snapshot on the steps outside the club, and to post a print to each man's family in Britain, with a note about the subject's happiness and health. We discovered that the United Services

Organisation performed a function which at home was shared by ENSA and the NAAFI, plus a little religion on the side — a weekly service known as "Vespers". It also ran "Variety Nights", and tea and supper dances at the Daniel Ashley Hotel on Ashley Street (where else?), admission fifty cents.

Major Langer, good and kind, was as typically American of his age and background as the peach-skinned, drawling girls and the crew-cut cadets were of their own. It wasn't their fault, it was mine, that I found the girls so tiresome and the cadets so uncongenial. I was missing all the English things — the damp, grey days and proper cups of tea, the quiet cricket grounds and their adjacent pubs, the oaks and elms and green, green fields; I was missing my mother and my father, even my sister, and girls like Sandy, who spoke of me by name, not as their "date", and didn't think of their kisses as major contributions to the Allied war effort. I missed having older people on the scene — not just aunts and uncles, but the parents of my friends, folk in shops and bus queues, and teachers, whose decent, solid influence, often disregarded, occasionally scorned, had done so much to shape my thoughts and the way I lived my life. In America, I seldom saw their like. If there were men and women over forty years of age, they must have stayed at home — their contribution to society made in younger years, they hid themselves from sight.

For a month, however, it wasn't only over-forties who eschewed the sweltering Valdosta streets: these were the Dog Days, so called, said some, because the sun rose at the same time as the Dog Star, or, as others said, because it was a favourite time, among the canine population, for catching rabies. In the Dog Days, it was locally believed, birds were too tired to sing, rattlesnakes would strike without their customary warning, chicks wouldn't hatch, sores heal, washing dry or crops grow.

Whatever other process they disrupted, the Dog Days did not stop flying at Moody Field. Wearing only shirt and slacks, a head-set and sun-glasses, we flew formation, pilot-navigation exercises, beam-approach, and instructors' check-rides, hour after hour, Dog Day after Dog Day, above a landscape that looked like an old, dry pie-crust. I felt perpetually sleepy; to be seated for a moment — anywhere but in a cockpit — was to fall into the arms of Morpheus at once. Of thirty-six hours in Valdosta on an Open Post, I spent twenty-four in bed, waking only for a glance at *Esquire* magazine. Big Andy Anderson, the Old Harrovian who shared the hotel room, loomed in with Coca-Cola and sank on to his bed. "And what, precisely," he asked, "are you giggling at?"

I threw the magazine across. The drawing showed a scene inside a theatre; on the stage, a group of elegant socialites loll about in every circumstance of luxury. In the audience an equally well-dressed gentleman is turning to the wondering couple immediately behind him. "Why, certainly people really live like that," he is remarking. "I live like that myself."

"Sorry, old boy," said Anderson, at last. "I don't get it."

"Nor do I. I just felt like a good giggle." Once more, I handed over the controls to good old Morpheus.

Next day, on an instrument cross-country exercise, Dennis had control, and we were in the air for longer than I had been before — certainly much longer than the detail should have taken. As I explained to Featonby, this was no fault of mine: my half of the route — Moody to Eufaula to Dothan — had taken sixty minutes, which was pretty well on schedule. Dennis, flying Dothan to Tallahassee to Moody, was less punctilious. He began by laying a compass course at 180 degrees to the intended track — a fundamental error known as setting red on black — and flew in that direction for some time before he noticed that where Tallahassee should have been was clearly somewhere else. Never quite recovering from that inauspicious start, he foozled all his radio bearings and, half-an-hour later, went round in circles on the Tallahassee beam while I sat beside his shrouded figure, twiddling my thumbs, willing but forbidden to assist. The duty of a co-pilot was specifically defined: to watch for other aircraft, high ground and thunderstorms and not to interfere with pilotage unless the mission was in peril.

"We're getting rather low on gas," Dennis said, perceptively, after three hours in the air. "I guess we'll go back to Dothan and take some on."

That took quite a while: Dothan was a busy single-engined flying school, and we had to take our turn for landing — and for fuel — with what seemed like several hundred AT-6s. At last we got into the air and set off on our weary way to Tallahassee once again.

I didn't fall asleep but, what with the warmth of the cabin and the drone of the engines, it wasn't easy to maintain peak alertness. Aware that the unhappy Dennis, sweating underneath the hood, depended on me to provide the roving eye, I indulged in some make-believe to stimulate the senses: we were flying a lone, daylight mission deep into Germany, a death or glory raid on the Reichstag in Berlin — never yet attacked. My job was to man the gun-turret, fingers on the triggers, and to search every corner of the sky for any type of fighter which might seek to distract us from our aim . . .

There were no Huns in the sun as the AT-17 neared Moody — only a skyful of advanced trainers, buzzing purposefully about their own affairs. Not that Dennis needed any Messerschmitts to keep him from his target — the hood, the panel and the dah-dit dit-dah of the wireless beam was quite enough for that. "You cunning devil, Dennis," I said at last. "I see what you're up to — you're going to fox them all at Moody by flying straight past and sneaking back in from the north."

"Oh, hell," said Dennis, losing the accent once again, "this bloody compass must be u/s. It's been swinging all over the place."

"I've noticed that sometimes — especially when the aircraft's swinging about all over the place."

"Shut up," snarled Dennis. "I'm concentrating."

"Pack it in, Dennis, you've done enough for honour and a dollar a day. You've been under the hood for nearly two hours, man. Come on out."

179

You had to say this for Dennis: he had the doggedness, if little else, that bomber pilots needed. "No fear," he muttered, "I'm going in on the beam." He wallowed on, while the signal gradually diminished in the head-phones. At last he spoke again. "Er — which way did you say the field was?"

I sighed with relief. "Due west, about three miles away."

We may not have been the first cadets at Moody to keep an AT-17 in the air for four hours, but we were certainly the last: both the Cessna and the Curtiss were being phased out of the programme. Their replacement was the Boeing Beechcraft AT-10 Wichita, which had the same Lycoming engines as the AT-9, but was a more responsive aeroplane to fly. Furthermore, it had the looks of an aeroplane, not a flying amoeba, like the AT-9, with its great rounded head and tiny tapered tail, nor of one that had been hastily constructed from parts of other aircraft, like the AT-17. If an aeroplane looked right, I was learning, the chances were that it would fly right.

But even the performance of the AT-10, which cruised at something better than 180 MPH at 10,000 feet, glided at 90 and touched down at a gentle 55, failed to satisfy the flying line cognoscenti. In their opinion, as I overheard, it should have been capable of giving the experience of flying a combat aeroplane.

"It don't fly fast enough," complained Lieutenant Carlson.

"It don't climb high enough," Lieutenant Fisher added.

"Moody's an Advanced School for twin-motored ships, right?" Lieutenant Heidrich demanded. "So how come the AT-6's engine is the only one on the base with any goddam power?"

"Yeah," Lieutenant Midkiff agreed, "an' I'm here to tell you that this AT-10 is one sonofabitch to put down in a cross-wind."

"An' how the Sam Hill do we teach bombardment in a ship with no bomb gear?"

"You wanna know why we gottem?" Lieutenant Heidrich continued. "The others have been breaking up all over Texas and California. Plywood, see? The Air Force figure they might hold together some place where it's kinda humid."

"Yeah, that figures, but let's wait an' see what the stoodents do to them . . . Hey, that Mister there! Get your ass outa here!"

It was Lieutenant Heidrich who checked me out on the replacement. The cabin layout was excellent, and the Sperry autopilot a revelation. Heidrich was one of five instructors with whom I flew at Moody, and this discontinuity was one of the less attractive features of the Advanced training. At least it was possible to develop a tenuous relationship with Heidrich — we ventured out together half-a-dozen times — and with Pilot Officer Walmsley of the RAF who, pale but determined, doubled Heidrich's record. Others, less courageous, found that one or two details were quite enough for them. Even with the persevering Walmsley there was never much rapport: for one thing, his flying made me almost as anxious as he was and, for another,

181

I didn't want his fate, like that of Ross at Souther, to rub off on me.

When the commissioning board sat in August, the President, glancing through my papers, gave an incredulous gasp. "Are you aware," he asked, "how many demerits you have earned in your kaydetship?"

"Not to the odd one or two, Sir. Only roughly."

"One hunnerd eighty, Mister, to the odd one precisely." He looked round at the other members of the board with the air of a man who has finally discovered the source of the nasty smell on the landing. "In my experience of officer candidates, gennulmen, which as you know is extensive, this guy stands alone." He leaned forward, and eyed me with interest. "Do you have any explanation for this — heh — this reccud?"

Several possible responses came to mind: "There must have been a clerical error, Sir", or "I'm the victim of injustice", even a candid, "Laziness, naughtiness and insubordination, Sir". I discarded them. The Colonel's question was probably rhetorical and, anyway, there was nothing to explain. "No, Sir."

The Colonel nodded. "No, indeed, I should say not. Okay, you walked your tours, and I guess you learned your lesson." He referred to the papers before him on the table. On the top of a cabinet behind him, an electric fan breathed heavily, turning this way and that, as though for air. "You made Kaydet Lootenant at Basic, I see. Do you like to fly, Currie?"

"Yes, Sir."

"Okay." He glanced at the second member of the board. "Major Franks?"

Franks, the senior British officer at Moody, was a Squadron Leader, but the USAAF, with a touch of chauvinism, habitually translated RAF ranks to their own. Beside the bristling crew-cuts of his colleagues, the fair wave of hair across the Squadron Leader's forehead gave him a boyish look compared with their maturity. He smiled when he spoke, and his voice was light, and pleasant. He asked which of the trainers I found best to fly, and I said I liked them all, but he pressed me for an answer, so I told him the AT-10. At that there was an exchange of nods along the table, which worried me a bit, because I didn't want to please them. The Squadron Leader asked what sort of aeroplanes I hoped to fly on operations, and when I told him he required a reason. I mentioned a long-held ambition to fly a heavy bomber and boldly added that I thought I was best suited to that sort of flying.

"Well, you've had above-average assessments here," he said, "so I should think you have a reasonable chance of getting what you want." Then came the crunch: "Of course, you might have to do a spell of instructing first." He sat back, and the Colonel turned to the USAAF Staff Captain, who smiled, but not quite so pleasantly as the Squadron Leader had. "A leedle tactical problem for you, Mister, okay?" he rasped. "You are first pilot of a bombardment ship, and you have the misfortune to experience total engine failure at low altitood. Right ahead of you are three buildings, and you sure as hell are gonna hit one of them. Best you can do is decide which." He paused, holding a

183

pencil delicately poised between his fingers. "Okay so far?"

"Yes, Sir." I was wondering what his idea of a big problem was.

"What these buildings are is number one, a hospital, number two, a kids' school and number three, a gaol. So which one do you hit?"

I wanted to tell him that ace bomber pilots just didn't get into those situations, but the expression on his face decided me against it. "I suppose it would be the prison, Sir."

"Suppose? You have no time for supposing."

"The gaol, Sir."

He stopped balancing the pencil, and made a note. "Okay, so you hit the gaol. You gonna tell the board why?"

"It seems to be the least of three evils."

"Too bad for the guys in there," he commented.

"Not too good for me and my crew, Sir."

Squadron Leader Franks gave a sympathetic chuckle, but the Captain didn't find himself amused. What had the worthy prison staff done, he required to know, or indeed the prisoners, paying their debt to society, that I should choose to end their lives? I said I was sorry about that, but they'd have to come third behind the doctors and the children.

"On that," said the Captain, examining the pencil-point with exaggerated care, "maybe you should have asked me what time of day it was . . ." I took his point — evening or night-time, a few doctors in the hospital, no children in the school. ". . . or maybe what time of year. I believe the schools are closed three months outa twelve." He put the pencil down as though putting me down with it, and with as little effort. "Why do you wanna be an officer, Currie?"

"I don't, Sir."

"How's that again?"

"Just one moment," the Colonel interrupted, "just one cotton-pickin' moment. Do I understand you don't *wanna* make officer?"

"Yes, Sir. I mean, no, Sir — I don't."

He glared at the Squadron Leader, the Captain and then again at me. "What the Sam Hill are you doing here, wasting the time of this Board?"

"I was detailed, Sir."

"Excuse me, Colonel," said Squadron Leader Franks, and I was glad of the excuse to look away from the slowly purpling face across the table. "Why don't you want to be commissioned?"

"I'm too young, Sir."

The Colonel checked a paper. "You are all of twenty years old, Mister."

"Yes, Sir. I asked my father about this, and his opinion was that no-one should be commissioned before the age of twenty-one."

"I made Second Lootenant when I was nineteen, Goddam it!"

"My father wouldn't have been thinking of Americans, Sir," I said, thinking fast. "We take longer to mature in England."

"That so?" He stared at me for a moment, and turned to Squadron Leader Franks. "Do you have

185

noncoms flying bombardment ships in the RAF, Major?"

"Oh, yes, Colonel. I should say the majority of pilots in Bomber Command are NCOs."

"Uh-huh." The narrow grey eyes were probing into my head. "Are you being entirely straight with this Board, Mister?"

I wanted to say "Absolutely, Sir", but that wasn't what came out. "There is a bit more to it than that, Sir."

He nodded. Now he would dig deeper and expose my simple strategy. If they — the all-powerful and implacable they — really needed instructors, they could give commissions willy-nilly and keep people in America, away from home and heavy bombers until the end of time. But I misjudged the man. He took a pack of cigarettes from the pocket of his shirt and peeled away a corner of the silver wrapping paper. "Get outa here, young feller," he said. "You have a recommendation for bombardment. Make good use of it."

CHAPTER ELEVEN

A Little Pair of Silver Wings

In the late afternoon of 30th August 1942, AT-10 No. 218 landed at Moody Field from a four-and-a-half hour cross-country exercise, taxied to the flying line and stopped. I pulled the pitch levers back, set the mixture to rich and let the engines idle until the fuel-pressure dropped. I cut the ignition and opened the throttles until the engines stopped then, with the "wobble-pump", fed fuel to the pipelines and the carburettors for the next student's flight. I turned the battery master-switch off. It was the last shut-down drill I would make as a student.

Writing up my log book for the final assessment, I rather wished that Dennis had been with me on that last cross-country, because he would surely have extended it by another sixty minutes, and that would have brought the total to exactly 250 hours. Of the 249, thirty-one had been at night, thirty-five on instruments, in seven types of aircraft. Precious hours and priceless experience, thanks to the mighty technical resources of the US Army Air Corps and the climate of Georgia.

187

Pilots trained in Canada, and at home in England, had to be satisfied with sixty or seventy hours less flying time and four or five fewer types. To my everlasting shame, I'd spent more hours walking tours than in the air.

Writing to my father, I admitted that I'd used his name in vain, although not unavailingly. I hoped he wouldn't be disappointed if I came home as a Sergeant and added: "I don't feel I have enough experience to give me any real authority, and I've always rather jeered at inexperienced officers coming straight from training into the responsibilities of a commission. The sudden authority didn't seem to do them much good. I plan to get my wings and three stripes, come home, get back into the RAF ways, go through an Operational Training Unit and, when I'm in my depth, I might feel justified in taking a commission — if it should be offered".

Next day, Featonby, Davison, Heppinstall, Anderson and I took the coach to Jacksonville, on Florida's east coast. We had six days' leave before Graduation Day — the first I'd had, for one reason or another, since I embraced my mother on the platform at Euston a hundred years ago.

We ate enormously, making fun of all the rules of West Point table etiquette, revelled in the luxury of staying late in bed, shopped around for little presents to take home to our folks, braved the Atlantic rollers (I, never far from Featonby), took in the movies and danced every night away.

It was on a solo mission to a night club that I encountered the Du Ponts, who came from St

Augustine, a few miles down the coast. Quickly discovering my total ignorance of Florida's history, they took pains to repair it, amusingly and well. The band was good, with a solid tempo, not too loud a volume and a leader who played trumpet in the style of Harry James. As the Du Ponts talked, sipping Whiskey Sours, and I the good Schlitz beer, the night wore on agreeably. I imagined the unlikely analogy of a casual meeting in, say, Bexhill, at which two young people entertained a stranger with as much as he could drink, plus a blow-by-blow account of the Norman conquest and its effect on their environment.

Ed Du Pont, it transpired, was in the hosiery business and, eliciting the fact that there were girls in England whose goodwill I valued, he promptly declared that a dozen pairs of the finest silk stockings would be mailed to Moody Field within the next twelve hours. While I was demurring — not too vehemently — the leader of the band approached the table, and Du Pont rose to shake him by the hand. "Joe," he said, "I want you to meet Aviation Cadet Jack Currie, from England. He's on furlough right now, and he tells me he likes Jacksonville real well except for one thing."

Dangling the silver trumpet in one hand and mopping a handkerchief across his brow with the other, Joe nodded. "Sure, Mr Du Pont, I know — my music, right?" He gave me a quick, practised smile. "Real good to know you, Sir. Okay if I introdooce you to the customers? They'll be glad to know we have an English flier right here in the club."

He raised a beckoning finger and a smiling girl brought him a microphone. "When I ask you what's your favourite toon," he said, out of the corner of his mouth, "tell me 'Sugar Blues.' Goddit, Jack?"

I'd never heard of the number, but that clearly couldn't matter less, so I said "Goddit", and the drummer played a roll. A spotlight glared down on the table while the affable Joe, with his arm round my shoulders, having openly confessed his admiration for the Royal English Air Force, announced my presence as its representative. How, he asked himself, could he best mark the occasion? He thrust the microphone towards me.

"Do you happen to know," I dutifully asked, "a tune called 'Sugar Blues'?"

He surely did, and would be happy to play it, especially for me. The spotlight followed him back to the band-stand, the customers clapped, calling out "Good luck" and "Happy landings", and I sank into my seat. Du Pont poured more Schlitz, with a sympathetic grin: the main ordeal was yet to come. Joe led the band through the introduction and first chorus, conducting from the hip with small movements of one finger. Then, pursued by his spotlight, with trumpet menacingly aimed, he advanced upon the table and proceeded to deliver the solo in my ear, while the Du Ponts sat and smiled on either side, and photographers' flash-bulbs popped all around us. It was only the requirement to uphold the traditions of the Royal English Air Force which prevented me from making my excuses and bolting for the loo.

At last, the solo reached a shattering crescendo, and "Sugar Blues" was done. Amid the crowd's renewed applause, Joe shook my hand again and, perspiring freely, took a bow. He departed with the habitual injunction: "You be sure to come back an' see us, real soon, you hear?"

The Du Ponts arranged a full social programme for the following two days, and it wasn't until the eve of our return to Valdosta that I rejoined my companions. We were comfortably located in a downtown hotel bar, drinking beer and swapping stories, when a sergeant air-gunner, wearing RAF khaki drill, approached our table. Insisting, in a strong Scottish accent, that no one stood on ceremony, and that all must call him "Mac", he bought a round of drinks which, at that stage of the furlough, was enough to assure him of our friendship for life. He was a gunnery instructor, he revealed, at an all-British single-engined school in Texas, presently enjoying a few days' leave, in company with "Mrs Mac", herself a native of the Lone Star State. This lady, on arrival, proved to be of buxom build, flamboyantly attired, with a liking for fun and Bourbon whiskey. She didn't so much join the party as enlarge it, and her voice — in the exercise of which she didn't spare herself — was capable of a pitch and volume Joe the Trumpet would have envied.

Soon, our little gathering became the focus of attention for the people in the bar. These now included a group of US Navy men, one of whom, attracted by her style, approached and, swaying slightly, asked Mrs Mac for the pleasure of a dance. She looked him up

191

and down and peremptorily declined the invitation, which the sailor then repeated with greater urgency if with no greater clarity of speech. She responded with an interesting suggestion as to how he might employ himself, and turned away. The sailor then declared that he himself was Texas born and, having recognised her accent, took the view that she would be better occupied with him than with a goddam bunch of goddam limeys. At this, the lady took considerable affront, and stated with some vehemence that her British husband, and his British friends, were gentlemen of a sort whose boots no lowlife, sassy naval rating — the word she used was "gob" — should flatter himself that he was fit to lick. They, she cried, had fought long years for freedom's cause, while he had pursued a degenerate career — her suggestion appeared to be that this included abusing himself and co-habiting with animals — and, what was more, she didn't like his face. The sailor answered with some asperity, which inspired Mrs Mac to further invective. Such of her language as originated in her own experience was salty enough, and it was made even sharper by what I recognised, from memories of Walker, as borrowings from the wealth of a Glaswegian vocabulary. Inevitably, an epithet was aired which could not but escalate the level of exchange from the verbal to the physical, and the lady invoked the Sergeant's aid as one who would let slip the dogs of war.

"Sock him, Mac," she bugled, "the bum insulted me!"

The sergeant's rock-like fist was striking as he rose. It hit the sailor between the eyes with a noise like a door

192

being slammed, and he fell heavily to the floor. Instantly, the space around the table was full of US Navy, spitting on their hands. Anderson set down his glass, sighed resignedly and, rising to his impressive six-feet-four, singled out the largest sailor for attention. I rose, less impressively, and reluctantly followed him into the fray. Sergeant Mac was lustily engaged in ensuring that his victim would give no more offence, and his lady, still in good voice, was laying about him shrewdly with a handbag. Featonby was giving the burly Heppinstall all support short of physical involvement, and Davison, prancing like an April lamb, was throwing fierce straight lefts in all directions. (Where were you, Garrett, when we needed you?)

Members of the hotel staff, for reasons of their own, were involving themselves in the affair, and the sound of battle quickly rose above the muted brass of Glenn Miller's orchestra, playing on the juke-box. Anderson had felled his man with a barrage of club-like blows, and now stood with his back against the wall, beset by three assailants. It was the work of a moment to tap the smallest of these on the shoulder and to punch him as he turned. The blow, imperfectly timed, struck the sailor's cheekbone, and nearly broke my knuckles. Frowning, the sailor shook his head, and threw his arms around my waist in an embrace not unlike that of the Macon man-trap, Cindy Lou. There, however, the likeness dissipated: Cindy Lou, to do her justice, had neither tried to kick me in the shins nor to beat my face in with her forehead. As I sought, by jumping from foot to foot and jerking my head from side to side, to avoid

193

these attentions, the sailor and I began to lurch across the floor in an eccentric dance.

Some strenuous moments passed in this performance, until I became aware, not only that the battle-noises had abated, but that my partner and I had all the room we needed for manoeuvre. It was like the moment in an Astaire movie when the people in the ballroom realise that he and Ginger Rogers are among them, and smilingly fall back to let them have the floor. Given the breath, it would have been the perfect music cue for "Must you dance, quite so close . . ." But it wasn't our artistry that had stilled the room: we had been decisively upstaged. The sailor's bear-hug fell away. "Shore Patrol," he snarled, out of one side of his mouth. "I'll see ya later, buddy."

At the top of the steps that led into the foyer stood two tall SPs of the US Navy, white-gloved, helmeted and gaitered, each with a truncheon in his hand. Two more, similarly equipped, guarded the entrance to the toilets. One of those on the stairway, casually swinging his truncheon and rocking gently on the balls of his feet, spoke in a harsh, authoritative drawl. "Okay, hear this, you men. This establishment is off limits to US Navy personnel, as of now. Let's go, on the double!"

Obediently, the sailors shuffled up the stairs, past the SPs and out into the night, leaving us among the upturned chairs and tables. As we massaged bruises, mopped eyes and straightened ties, the senior SP, head thrown back to show cold, blue eyes beneath the peak cap, addressed himself to Sergeant Mac. "Are you-all fixin' to ree-side in this establishment overnight, Sergeant?"

"Aye, that's right. The wife and I have a room here."

"Okay, fine. How's about you other guys?"

I told him where our rooms were, about a mile away. The SP nodded. "I figure it'd be a good idee for you-all to stick around a while if'n you wanna stay outa trouble. The Navy's in town, an' you-all are kind of outnumbered."

He swung on his heel and, followed by his cohorts, swaggered through the door. Sergeant Mac found his cigarettes on the floor and offered them around. He clapped Anderson on the back and grinned at the rest of us. "Thanks for the help, you people. Per ardua ad astra, eh? Now, we're all away up to our room for a cup of coffee and a wee dram."

We demurred politely, he and Mrs Mac insisted, and from their bedroom window we saw the reason why. The sailors were waiting in the street below, leaning in the doorways, squatting on the sidewalk, chewing gum and passing bottles. Their numbers grew as further parties joined them. "Too many of the boogers for us," Heppinstall whispered in my ear. "I wish Mac's woman had danced with the sod — we'd be tucked up in bed by now." It was two o'clock in the morning before we ventured out and tiptoed through the silent streets to our hotel.

So that brief, long-awaited leave drew near its end in an atmosphere of slapstick. I didn't know that the last act would be farce, I only knew I had to see the play through to the end. While the others made their way back to Moody, with a view to pressing slacks and shining shoes for Graduation, I opted for one last fling in town — and where better could a final fling be flung than at the Daniel Ashley dance? Wheedling three dollars out of Featonby, and weathering the shower of Polonius-style moralising that accompanied them, I zeroed in on Valdosta's Ashley Street.

The trouble was, the people at the bar were so friendly, the bar-stool so comfortable and the booze so drinkable, that a certain element of rot set in. I lapped alternate Whiskey Sours and Budweiser beers until the voice of a girl, singing with the band, evoked that well-known feeling.

"Skylark, have you anything to say to me,
Won't you tell me where my love can be?
Is there a meadow in the mist,
Where someone's waiting to be kissed . . ."

Through the slightly swimming scene on the dance-floor, a face I recognised appeared; it was the face of Thelma, the waitress with the bubble-cut at the Moody Post Exchange. I raised a happy hand and she flashed her eyes across her partner's shoulder.

It was surprisingly easy to get down from the stool, but a little more difficult to walk across the floor — dancing couples would keep getting in the way. Momentarily baffled, I halted at a table. It was impossible to focus on anyone among the moving throng, but another drink would be sure to clear my head. As luck would have it, there were several half full glasses right there on the table.

"Skylark, I don't know if you can find these things,
But my heart is riding on your wings,
So if you see them anywhere,
Say, won't you lead me there?"

The throb of music ended, the dancers drifted from the floor. Some came to the table and began to talk about the empty glasses. I explained the focusing problem, but they didn't seem to understand, so I asked them to excuse me and set off on a square search of the floor. Although it was much easier without the couples to bump into, the floor itself had become quite sharply tilted, and it was really quite hard to walk in a straight line. In any event, the search was fruitless: Thelma was nowhere to be seen.

Getting back on to the bar-stool was a lot more difficult than getting off, but I managed it after a while and ordered a Budweiser, which the barman wanted money for, although I told him several times that I was a qualified pilot. I fell to brooding on the mystery of girls — particularly of Thelma, who had disappeared precisely at the moment she was needed. She was undoubtedly the prettiest of all the PX girls, and now I would probably never see her again. Sadness began to set in. Graduation Day tomorrow, the climax of two years' training, and here I was — utterly alone. No girl, no friends, no money. I hadn't wept since I was quite a little boy: this seemed like a good time to take it up again. I laid my head down on the bar, and was trying to remember the starting drill for weeping, when I noticed a pile of coins — nickels, dimes and quarters — inches from my nose. The fates had smiled: a fellow needed money, they instantly provided it. I ordered more Budweiser and pocketed the change. I was asking the barman what he thought of girls with bubble-cuts who flashed their eyes at people and then just disappeared, when a swarthy man in a dinner-jacket tapped me on the arm. "Pardon me, soldier," he said, "did you-all pick up my change, by any chance?"

I started to tell him how it felt to be a qualified pilot who couldn't find a girl, but he interrupted, complaining that I was spilling beer on his tuxedo and, when I got off the stool to dry him with a handkerchief, he called out loudly that I was standing on his foot. He really was rather a moaner. I stepped off his foot as quickly as I could and fell over the stool against the customer behind me. He turned out to be a moaner, too. In fact, that end of the bar was getting to be thick with moaners. I decided to move on a bit, but some of my feet had become entangled with the stool. I would have fallen heavily if the swarthy man hadn't been underneath.

Two more men helped me up — large, heavy-breathing men with hands like grappling-irons. We moved along together very well, those men and I, without the slightest effort on my part, through a kaleidoscope of tables, lights and smiling faces. The swing-doors into Ashley Street flew open, and I slid across the sidewalk on my stomach. I pulled myself erect by the door-handle of a cab, which happened to be standing at the kerb.

"Where to, buddy?" said the driver.

I rubbed my arm. It felt numb, but probably not broken in more than two places. My collar was torn, several shirt-buttons had gone, and the tie would never be the same again. There was a sore place on the part of my head that had been used to open the doors. "I've lost my cap," I said.

"Too bad, buddy. Where to?"

"I think I'm going to be sick."

"Goodnight, buddy" He leaned out of the window and pushed me away. Suddenly, Valdosta seemed to be full of people with nothing better to do than pull me or push me around. A feeling of resentment overcame the nausea. I clenched the fist of the good arm, and was drawing it back when someone grasped me round the waist from behind. It really was extraordinary — these wrestlers were everywhere. I seized a wrist and wrenched it away. The wrist was smooth, and slim. I turned. The wrist belonged to Thelma.

"Take it easy, Mister," she said. "Let's don't git in no more trouble."

"What happened to you, Thelma? I made a searchless fruit for you in there."

"I had to tell my date goodnight. Hey, you-all are on Graduation Parade in the morning — do you have the cab-fare to Moody?"

"It's all right, I'll catch the bus."

She raised her eyes to heaven and pursed her lips, which I promptly kissed. "Cut that out, fresh. You-all know what time it is? The last bus left two hours ago."

"That's awkward." I pondered for a moment. "I say, Thelma . . ."

"Don't ask me, Mister. Sure, I would if I could, but I'm flat, too."

The cab-driver tilted his cap over his eyes and lay back in the seat. Thelma took my arm and led me along the sidewalk. During the evening, one of my legs had grown longer than the other, which produced a tendency to veer to starboard. It was only the steady pull of Thelma's little hand that kept me out of the shop doorways. She looked into my face and giggled. "Boy, are you loaded! Why don't you straighten up an' fly right?"

"Don't worry, Thelma. It's nothing that a three-hour walk won't cure."

"How's that again?"

"Just point me in the right direction."

"No, sir. You-all gotta git some nod afore you go on that parade. You take the first bus in the morning."

The thought of sleep was like a whiff of chloroform. My eyelids closed and the knee of the shorter leg began to buckle. Thelma held on. "Will you promise to be good if'n I take you back to my place?"

"No."

"Okay, the deal's off. Start walkin'."

"All right, I'll be good. Where do you live, Thelma?"

"Three blocks from here. I guess I'll have to let you-all in through the window. An' don't make no

200

racket, for Pete's sake, or I'll be in big trouble with th\
Hackenschmitts."

"With the what?"

"The folk who own the place — they live on the second floor back."

I waited on the porch, swaying, while the night breathed hot around me. When Thelma pushed the window-shutters open, I crawled in like a cat-burglar with a bad bout of arthritis. Her shoulders gleamed and her breasts lifted as she put her arms around my neck, and pulled my head down for her to kiss. When I closed my eyes the room began to swing, and the only way to stop it was by concentrating on doing something difficult, like unbuttoning her dance-frock.

We had to cuddle close together in the bed, because that was the only way of staying in it. A sainted, paralysed octogenarian could not but have responded to the call of glowing skin, sweet lips, soft hair. The bed creaked like a rusty bicycle, and I hoped that Mr and Mrs Hackenschmitt were heavy sleepers.

"You-all promised to be good," she whispered.

"I'm trying to be, but I'm awfully weak."

When I woke, the room was lit by bars of sunlight. The time was half-past six, the early bus had gone an hour ago and the second would even now be drawing out of town. I pulled on my shirt and slacks and tumbled through the window into the blinding day. I caught the 7.45 and was in the nick of time to join the ranks of 42H before they trooped into the Graduation hall.

"Holy smoke!" said Featonby. "You look awful. Where's your cap?"

"You'll have to lend me yours. Don't worry, you can have it back for your turn."

Featonby's cap seemed larger and sharper-edged than mine, and the buttons twinkled brighter than the Gemini. To wear it was almost to assume a new personality. I would have liked to live up to Featonby's cap, but it was far too late to think of that.

My perception of the parade preliminaries was seriously impaired — partly by an incipient headache, but largely by a total lack of breakfast. When the Chaplain invoked divine assistance with the ceremony, I would have supported him more earnestly if it hadn't been for the crisp bacon-rashers and eggs-over-easy that were sizzling in my thoughts; the Director of Training's opening address had to compete with grilled Wiener sausages and Hominy grits; while the Commandant of Cadets administered the oath of dedication, I moved on to syrup-covered waffles and a gallon of black coffee. Somewhere far away, the name of Adams was called, then that of Anderson. As though waking for a second in the middle of a dream, I saw Andy tramping up the steps, saw the Director of Training reaching up to pin the shining wings upon his chest, but when Clipsham stepped forward I was back among the waffles — this time with double cream.

"Wakey, wakey," hissed Davison, "you're next."

The Director took another badge from his aide, and turned with an automatic smile. Stepping close, he pinched a small fold in my shirt over the breast-pocket,

202

and inserted the pin. At that point, he paused. His eyes, inches from mine, roved, recoiled and roved again — like two nomadic beetles on an unfamiliar wall. In them, I saw his thoughts: "This guy has no buttons on his shirt — no, that's not possible — wait though, it's true — not a goddam button!"

Still holding the badge, but not the smile, he took in the remainder of the scene — the dilapidated tie, the lipstick on the collar, the Bourbon on the shirt. Ranging higher, his gaze embraced the stubbly chin, the door-opener forehead and the bloodshot eyes. His own eyes had no blood in them at all — just ice. Was it in his power, I wondered, even now to snatch those silver wings away, and to sentence me to walking tours for ever more?

"Excuse me, Sir," I whispered, "you're sticking the pin in my chest."

"I know that, Mister. I wanna check that you're real."

He fixed the pin into the clasp and shook my clammy hand in his, which was hard and dry, before he spoke again. It was noticeable that he did this without unclenching his teeth. "Congratulations, Currie . . ."

"Thank you, Sir."

The Director hadn't finished. He continued, speaking softly, as softly as a chain-saw cutting through a log, ". . . on graduating, not — repeat not — on your turn-out. You look as though you were just thrown out of some low-down, Goddam honky-tonk."

"The Daniel Ashley Hotel, actually, Sir."

"That so? Well, I'm sure glad you could spare the time to come along today."

"Wouldn't have missed it for anything, Sir."

The Director squared his shoulders. Was it that the ice in his eyes had fractionally melted, or that mine were watering from too much standing at attention? "Good luck, Mister," he grated. "I believe you're gonna need it."

Passing the exemplary cap back to Featonby, I felt a sense of déjà vu. Four years earlier, at the School Speech Day, when the great Field Marshal Allenby had handed out the prizes, I'd somehow got the timing wrong and was made up as Shylock for the Merchant's trial scene — which Form V was to offer later in the programme. "No, boy," the junior English master had said, "you will certainly not go up for your prize wearing a false nose and a beard. That would be quite unsuitable, and it might upset Lord Allenby. Weston will receive it for you. And stop making faces — your nose will come unstuck."

Ever since then, an atmosphere of bathos had marked the most portentous moments in my life, and the syndrome would persist — when, a year or so later, my turn came for an award, King George VI knew better than to have me at the Palace — he had them send it to me through the mail. At least, I'd been present to receive my wings — but I wished the Director hadn't pinned them to my skin.

CHAPTER
TWELVE

And so to the Lancaster

Two months passed in waiting, travelling and more waiting: three days on the train back to Moncton — "Get rid of those Yankee trinkets," barked the RCAF Flight Sergeant in the stores, as he passed the woven brevets of the RAF across the counter — three weeks of boredom (apart from the reunion with Walker and Treadaway) before the passage home, and six days to cross the ocean in the sort of armada of which Percy Burt had dreamed at Milford Haven ten months ago. But it wasn't only the size of the convoy, nor its speed, which made the voyage so different from the earlier experience. Then, if Class 42H, as aircrew under training, had gone to the bottom of the Atlantic, only our nearest and dearest would have missed us; now, we could fly, and the Squadrons needed us: Britain had invested a lot in our training, and was protecting the investment.

No one slung a hammock aboard the *Stirling Castle*, and someone else did the chores. We slept in bunks and dined in state — as though in a West End restaurant afloat. There was air protection, too.

We were standing at the taffrail amidships, working up an appetite for lunch, and watching the destroyers shepherding the cargo-ships, when Anderson pointed at the eastern sky ahead. Three or four miles away, at 6,000 feet or so, a large aircraft was making a slow, wide orbit. "Focke-Wulf Condor," said Walker promptly, "a long-range recce. The sod'll be radioing our position to a sub."

"Not for long, mate," shouted Garrett, "look at that!" From the deck of the US Navy cruiser in the convoy's midst, a rugged little fighter was catapulted into the air. As it climbed in a bee-line to the east, Davison anticipated Walker by a split second. "Chance-Vought Corsair," he shrilled. The Condor broke off its orbit and, chased by the fighter, disappeared from sight. The Corsair, having seen off the intruder, returned some twenty minutes later, splashed down beside the cruiser and commenced, slowly but remorselessly, to sink. At the last moment, however, when only the rudder, canopy and one propeller-blade were protruding from the waves, a derrick on the cruiser's deck plucked it from the water and lifted it on board. It was an exercise to marvel at, and we cheered it to the echo, but, as one of nature's sinkers, I was glad I hadn't trained at Pensacola.

The long, green sweep of the Irish coastline looked peaceful and serene in the October sun, as though untouched by war: it was the sight of Liverpool's disfigurement and Birkenhead's scars that told us we were home. Everyone on deck was rather quiet as the *Stirling Castle* steamed up the Mersey — quiet, but content. I, for one, had seldom felt so happy. I didn't even fret when I discovered, on the quay, that some light-fingered character had known exactly where to find those little presents for the family, wrapped and ready in a kitbag in the hold. That sort of mishap was part of coming home.

We travelled by train down the lovely length of England, with autumn's colours waving in the trees, for another three weeks of waiting in a Bournemouth hotel, stripped of all but the essentials for vulgarians like us. Just along the coast lived friends of the family, quick to provide a lodging for my Mother and Father, and later for Sandy, when they came to see me. If I'd been to boarding school instead of being a day-boy, I would have been accustomed to being away from my parents for months at a time, and would have known what to expect. As it was, I was amazed that neither of them seemed to have aged, although I felt as though I'd been away a lifetime. Sandy hadn't changed a bit, either, still strong and tender, and a bit of a tomboy. Between cuddles, I told her about Sheff and the Lieutenant, and of Featonby, Walker, McLeod and the others. I didn't mention girls, and she didn't ask me. I was glad of that.

On 7th November, I was in the air again, flying an Airspeed Oxford at the Advanced Flying Unit, Shawbury. The lesson to be learned there, and at the satellite field, Condover, was that to find your way about in English winter skies was a very different matter from riding the radio-range over Georgia. At Condover, I was re-united with a founding member of the Stratford Seven, the ineffable Mugsy Johnson, who slept fully dressed in our icy Nissen hut and, waking in the night, knelt on my recumbent body (I had the bed by the window) to release the contents of his bladder without venturing outdoors.

Halfway through the course, there came a week of flying the beam at Newton, near Nottingham, where the Sergeants' Mess was as full of Polish aircrew as the Oxford's RT was of dots and dashes. Those twelve hours of solid SBA ranked as the most eardrum-crunching, mind-numbing hours of my life.[1] Then, it was back to muddy Condover for a few more cross-countries, in a fortnight enhanced by two days and nights with Sandy in the dark enchantment of a Shrewsbury hotel. While we were making love, Dave Garrett died. He tried very hard to escape from the cockpit of a burning Oxford, but failed.

In the final fragmentation of the Stratford friends, Featonby remained in Flying Training Command, while Davison was posted to Transport Command. Walker and Johnson went to Bomber OTUs, and so did I.

---

[1] Author's note: They still do.

88 Whitmore Road,
Harrow.
10 Jan 43

Sgt. Pilot Currie, J.A.L. 1337791,
Sergeants' Mess, No. 27 OTU,
RAF Station Lichfield, Staffs.

My dearest,
So glad to hear from you and all your interesting news, which is read over and over again. I gather you are feeling more settled with the Aussies and I hope you feel more comfortable about them as your crew. They all sound all right, anyway — especially your navigator. Do you find them easy to get on with and good airmen? How do you account for Ron being made an instructor? I always rather hoped you would be one, but I have lately heard that it isn't *such* a safe job, and I daresay it's monotonous. What is the the food like, dear? I hope you're getting plenty — and good warm food in this bitter weather. Is there anything you want knitting? What about a commission?

Always your loving Mother.

RAF Lichfield
15 Jan 43

Dear Mummy,

Many thanks for your letter. I also heard from Ron today, and he doesn't seem terribly enthusiastic about his present job. I sense a little envy of me and my Wellington. As for the selection of instructors, that seems to be according to their capabilities, character, and recommendations. The older men are usually made instructors unless they express a definite wish to do operational work. The instructor has to fly every hour of every day, weather permitting, and put up with the same stupid mistakes from pupil after pupil. His is the responsibility when a pupil goes solo, and his own flying must always be perfect, for a pupil copies everything he does. I think I shall be a good bomber pilot, but I haven't got the patience to be a good instructor. I should only be able to teach a chap how to fly as well as I do, whereas a good instructor should teach his pupil to fly better than he can. Ron, I think, could do that.

I shan't know whether I'm right about myself until I've been over a German target and heard the bomb-aimer say "bombs gone". I'll tell you how I feel about it then. The food is excellent, so please don't worry about that. It's very good of you to say you'll knit me something, especially a commission (!), but I'll settle for socks.

Your loving son.

88 Whitmore Road,
Harrow.
15 Feb 43

Sgt. Pilot Currie, J.A.L. 1337791,
Sergeants' Mess,
RAF Station, Church Broughton,
Derbyshire.

My dear boy,
I was very glad to hear about your crew and I trust
that you will work up into a good team — you
know, on the Yorkshire lines. I am pleased you are
getting to like the Wellingtons in spite of them
being rather heavy to handle. Probably with more
experience this heaviness will not be so apparent.
From what I can make out they seem to be one of
the most reliable 'planes in service. As you may
know we are having a Wings for Victory week; in
Trafalgar Square we have a Lancaster. It is really a
magnificent machine. It has been erected on site,
so most days I have spent a few minutes watching
the progress made. It has been on 27 raids, 2 of
which were in daylight. I have wished many times
that you were at home to explain the various parts
— still one day you may fly one and then you can
tell me about it.

Good luck,
Lots of love,
Daddy.

211

I did fly the Lancaster, a few weeks later, with those same Aussies and three of my own countrymen. We flew and fought together many times, and had a lot of luck. But that, as they say, is another story.[1]

---

[1] (Told in detail in LANCASTER TARGET by Jack Currie (paperback). The Publisher.)

Also available in ISIS Large Print:

Torpedo Leader

Wg Cdr Patrick Gibbs, DSO, DFC and BAR

"A squadron's missing pilots were never seen as a lengthening funeral column, a continual reminder of danger and bad luck, but as a band of friendly ghosts who stood on the tarmac as aircraft took off, smiling encouragement. They were remembered as living, flying and fighting; never thought of as dead."

Written during the war without benefit of hindsight, this is a remarkable and valuable account. A very personal story, its lucid, exciting and readable narrative describes firstly Patrick Gibbs' frustrations as a Staff Officer in Cairo, then his triumphs and disasters as a Beaufort Flight Commander on the anti-shipping operations from Malta in 1942, during which his contribution was immense, having realised that targeting enemy shipping was the key to victory.

ISBN 978-0-7531-9560-4 (hb)
ISBN 978-0-7531-9561-1 (pb)

I Sank the Bismarck

Lieutenant Commander John Moffat
with Mike Rossiter

"Although I seemed to get into all sort of scrapes, I enjoyed life; I remember the fun and excitement of various incidents rather than the tears that followed."

May 1941: the pilots of fifteen canvas-covered biplanes struggle to hold their Swordfish aircraft steady as they head towards the German battleship *Bismarck*, the most powerful warship in service anywhere in the world.

The mighty *Bismarck*'s guns fired a storm of shells and bullets at the approaching planes, but they flew on. Amongst them was a young sub-lieutenant in the Fleet Air Arm, John Moffat. The *Bismarck* was hit, lost control and steamed in circles until the ships of the Royal Navy could close in, allowing HMS *Dorsetshire*, to deliver the coup de grâce. Only years later was John told that the records suggested it was his torpedo that prevented the *Bismarck* from outrunning her pursuers.

ISBN 978-0-7531-9556-7 (hb)
ISBN 978-0-7531-9557-4 (pb)

Spitfire: A Test Pilot's Story

Jeffrey Quill

"... had a book of pictures of aeroplanes which I studied avidly. Occasionally — great excitement — real aeroplanes would fly overhead and my brothers and I would watch them intently until they were out of sight."

Starting with lively descriptions of the Royal Air Force in the mid-1930s, Jeffrey Quill moves on to cover his fascinating test flying experiences where he took charge of some of the most important military aircraft of that time. In particular, he flight-tested every variant of the immortal Spitfire, from its experimental, prototype stage in 1936 when he worked with its chief designer, R. J. Mitchell, to the end of its production in 1948. Using his first-hand experience of combat conditions fighting with 65 Squadron at the height of the Battle of Britain, Jeffrey Quill helped to turn this elegant flying machine into a deadly fighter aeroplane.

ISBN 978-0-7531-9548-2 (hb)
ISBN 978-0-7531-9549-9 (pb)

Ghosts of Targets Past

Philip Gray

"I couldn't help thinking that the Royal Air Force had a real problem on its hands. How did they figure on making a front-line, gung-ho pilot out of the sort of material I provided — a shy, reticent, non-belligerent country boy?"

Born in Scotland, Philip Gray is now a journalist living in Canada, but in WW2 he found himself captain of the crew of a "mighty Lanc", operating with 186 Squadron as the RAF took war right into the heart of Germany. Both Gray and his crew felt they were in charge of the undisputed king of the skies, but dangers lurked around every corner and on every mission. In an engaging yet frank style, Gray reveals the true relationships between himself and his team, and between the team members themselves. He also searches his own soul as he struggles to survive in love and war.

ISBN 978-0-7531-9542-0 (hb)
ISBN 978-0-7531-9543-7 (pb)

Escaper's Progress

David James

"Never had I foreseen that the enemy's fire would be so literally like a curtain; a safety curtain to him, since for us to fire torpedoes with any hope of success we had to see the target."

David James was serving in Motor Gun Boats when he was captured in February 1943. Imprisoned initially in Dulag Marlag, he immediately decided to escape. His first tunnel was discovered before completion. In December 1943 he succeeded in escaping and was on the run for almost a week disguised as an officer of the Royal Bulgarian Navy. He was captured while attempting to board a ship at Lubeck.

Undeterred, in February 1944 he broke out again, this time dressed as a Swedish sailor. Travelling by train to Bremen, Hamburg, Lubeck, Rostock and Danzig, he eventually succeeded in reaching Stockholm after two and a half days in a ship's engine room.

ISBN 978-0-7531-8380-9 (hb)
ISBN 978-0-7531-8381-6 (pb)